I.S.A.M. Monographs: Number 1

United States Music

RICHARD JACKSON

I.S.A.M. Monographs: Number 1

United States Music

SOURCES OF BIBLIOGRAPHY AND COLLECTIVE BIOGRAPHY

RICHARD JACKSON

//

Institute for Studies in American Music

Department of Music
Brooklyn College
of The City University of New York

Published by Institute for Studies in American Music,
Department of Music, Brooklyn College of the City University of New York
Brooklyn, New York 11210

INTRODUCTORY NOTE

The bibliography. I have compiled this list of books as a practical aid to students engaged in American-music studies. Since these studies are still relatively new in university music curricula, the need for such a list is real enough. My concentration here on sources of bibliography concerning various aspects of music in the United States and on sources of collective biographical information is a result of my daily contact with students at The New York Public Library.

"Where can I find a good list of books and articles on country-and-western?"

"Other than the Howard book, where can I find information on late 19th-century American composers?"

"I'm looking for violin and piano music composed by Americans before 1815. How do I find it?"

These are the kinds of questions most asked by those seeking ideas for term papers and other projects or, indeed, those at work on theses and dissertations.

Each book in this list (including some composed largely of pictures) contains at least one feature that contributes to the areas cited in the subtitle of this bibliography. If a book is concerned primarily with historical or critical commentary and analysis, I do not include it, fine though it may be. And I do not include certain other well-known books if I felt that some other book on the same subject, though less famous, contributes more fruitfully to my areas of concentration. On the other hand, a few well-known though essentially trashy books have been included because of the limited over-all coverage available in their subject areas. Finally, among the books on the list are some I do not specially care for, hence the presence of an occasional disagreeable annotation. Nevertheless, all the books listed have potentially useful features.

I have not cited general music reference works such as *Grove's Dictionary* (I have, however, listed its *American Supplement*), *The Music Index*, or *Baker's Biographical Dictionary*. I have assumed that the college-level music student is already familiar with these works and will recognize their potential application to his studies in United States music. Do I assume too much? (N.B. I will point out here one of my pet peeves with *Baker's*. It seems that Nicolas Slonimsky, the dictionary's indefatigable and justly celebrated editor, simply cannot resist indulging in malicious fun with performers in American popular

v

music. His articles on Frank Sinatra, Bing Crosby, and others are just too cute for words. They are also condescending and occasionally nasty. Do not look to this source for straightforward information on performers in this category.)

Citations and additional data. I have included all important printed matter on the title page—author(s), with name(s) given exactly as on title page; author of introduction (if other than the author of the book); full title (capitalization as on title page); subtitle and/or descriptive phrases (shortened only in cases of wildly abnormal length); place of publication (if it can be located in the book); publisher; date (even though not always located on the title page)—and the following descriptive elements (as pertinent): number of numbered pages (in Roman and Arabic numerals if so used in the book) or number of volumes or both; illustrations, plates, photographs; appendices; bibliography and/or discography (one book has a rollography!); indices; special features; series title, if any. If a descriptive phrase on a title page indicates "40 beautiful photographs in glowing black-and-white" and I have included this as part of the entry, I do not repeat "photos" among the descriptive elements; in fact, I do not repeat any information in this manner.

After the descriptive elements I have indicated the existence of a reprint and its publisher in this way: (R Johnson) This means that Johnson Reprint Corporation has issued a reprint edition of the work.

In addition, if I was able to locate reviews of a book, I indicate one or more, in this way: (reviewed *Musical Quarterly* 40:421-24 July 1954). This means that the review is to be found in volume 40 of *The Musical Quarterly*, the July 1954 issue, on pages 421 to 424.

In certain cases, I have listed separately various editions of a book, with descriptive elements, if I consider this information potentially useful or important. Generally, however, I have cited only latest editions.

Since I despise abbreviations, I have used as few as possible. Those that I have used most frequently (photos, intro, rev. ed., etc.) are too obvious to need explanation.

My special thanks to my friend and fellow-bibliographer Mel Schuster for his most valuable work on the preparation of the manuscript, and to my colleague Pamela Berlin for her assistance in tracking down fugitive data.

Richard Jackson

CONTENTS

I

REFERENCE WORKS

1   **Bio-bibliographical Index of Musicians in the United States of America Since Colonial Times** . . . [Title also in Spanish and Portuguese] Prepared by the District of Columbia Historical Records Survey, Division of Community Service Programs, Work Projects Administration; Sponsored by the Board of Commissioners of the District of Columbia; Cosponsors: Pan American Union, Library of Congress. Washington, D.C.: Music Division, Pan American Union, June 1941 xxiii, 439p forewords (by Charles Seeger; by Harold Spivacke) intro (by H.B. Dillard) [All prefatory matter in English, Spanish, and Portuguese] appendix ("A list of special studies, biographies, and autobiographies pertaining to the persons whose names appear in the Index") p421-39 (Music Series No. 2)

———————————————————. 2nd ed. 1956 [Minor changes in the title page; no series title] (R Da Capo Press)

"This Index was first planned in 1936 by Keyes Porter, who supervised the work until August 1939, when it lapsed temporarily. It was revived and expanded in January 1940 under the supervision of Dr. Leonard Ellinwood, and the sponsorship of the Library of Congress"—(introduction). The **Index** is the richest single source for locating information on people active in music in the United States before 1939. The original editions are paperback with text reproduced from typescript, a modest format which belies the importance of the content.

There are over 10,000 entries arranged in double columns per page. Each entry contains the following information: name (in the fullest form that could be located), dates (verified wherever possible), profession (composer, organ-builder, harpist, etc.), references to the books (with page numbers) where information may be found. An asterisk before a name indicates that the person was foreign-born. Since a majority of the 66 books indexed do not have individual indices, most of the data was not easily accessible prior to the publication of this work.

Despite its great utility, the **Index** does have limitations. The most serious are the scant representation of people in 20th-century popular music and the all but total absence of names in folk music and jazz. The omissions are due, in part, to the fact that the pop and folk fields were not well documented in book form before 1939. However, there were books on jazz available, so the omission of musicians in this field was apparently intentional.

Black musicians in general are not adequately represented in the **Index**. At least two substantial pre-1939 works on black music might have been indexed, Trotter's **Music and Some Highly Musical People (43)** and Cuney-Hare's **Negro Musicians and Their Music (39)**, but either by design or oversight they were not included. The few blacks who did get listed are identified as such, i.e. John Rosamond Johnson is a "Negro composer, director," Paul Robeson is a "Negro singer," and so on. This practice is, at the very least, controversial.

A note on the "Second Edition": this designation is misleading since the content is identical to that of the 1941 edition, no new books were indexed, and a few noticeable mistakes were not corrected. The 1956 version should be considered simply a second printing.

2 CHENEY, SIMEON PEASE The American Singing Book . . .   Boston: White, Smith and Co., 1879 320p preface indices (of tunes; of biographies)

An unusually interesting tunebook containing biographies of over forty "leading devotees in the work—the toilers, singers, composers and book makers, who have gone on to higher life, from William Billings to I. B. Woodbury"—(preface). As the title page suggests, the biographical section is "a valuable feature . . . which alone is worth the price of the book." Several scholars, George Hood and John W. Moore among them, are credited with assisting Cheney on the sketches; there are quotes from contemporary newspaper articles and letters of composers and their relatives. Some errors but generally very good.

The biographical section includes:

Billings, William	Keller, Matthias
Bradbury, William	Kimball, Jacob
Brown, Bartholomew	Kingsley, George
Browne, Augusta	Loder, George
Colburn, Marcus	Mason, Lowell
Cole, John	Maxim, Abraham
Doolittle, Eliakim	Moore, H. E.
Edson, Lewis	Moore, J. W.
Gould, Nathaniel	Morgan, Justin
Greatorex, Henry	Muhlenberg, W. A.
Harmon, Joel	Philips, Austin
Hastings, Thomas	Prouty, Elijah
Hayter, A. N.	Read, Daniel
Hill, U. C.	Sage, William
Hodges, Edward	Sanger, Zedekiah
Holden, Oliver	Sloman, Jane
Hood, George	Swan, Timothy
Hopkins, John H.	Watson, Henry
Holyoke, Samuel	West, Elisha
Ingalls, Jeremiah	Woodbury, I. B.
Janes, Walter	Zeuner, Charles
Jenks, Stephen	

3 **Current Biography** vol. 1, 1940–   New York: H. W. Wilson, 1940–   Published
monthly (except August); annual cumulation titled *Current Biography Yearbook*
photos

This extremely valuable biographical tool includes newsworthy personalities of various
nationalities and professions. Its coverage of figures involved in most aspects of United
States musical life since 1940 is surprisingly wide: composers, scholars, pop and jazz
performers, opera singers, librettists, critics, conductors—even a librarian or two. The
articles are well researched (sources are indicated), usually accurate, and of some depth;
a photo and address accompany each piece. The editors occasionally up-date articles;
they also include obituaries.

Though each *Yearbook* contains a certain amount of cumulative indexing, it can be somewhat troublesome to locate an article (especially if the subject has been given more than one, plus an obituary). For this reason, and because I feel that **Current Biography** is one of the best sources of contemporary coverage, I give here a comprehensive index (not a complete one), for 1940-70, of the biographies potentially most useful to the student of music in the United States.

Samples: Burleigh, Harry T.   41 49   [In *Yearbooks* 1941 and 1949 will be found
articles on Burleigh, in this case a biography and an obituary]

Cage, John   61   [In *Yearbook* 1961 the Cage article appears]

Cantor, Eddie   41 54 65   [In *Yearbooks* 1941, 1954, and 1965 Cantor
articles will be found, in this case two biographies and an obituary]

Adderley, Cannonball   61
Aldrich, Richard   42
Alpert, Herb   67
Anderson, Leroy   52
Anderson, Marian   40 50
Anka, Paul   64
Antheil, George   54 59
Armstrong, Louis   44
Arnold, Eddy   70
Autry, Gene   47

Babbitt, Milton   62
Bacharach, Burt   70
Baez, Joan   63
Bailey, Pearl   55 69
Baker, Josephine   64
Ballard, Kaye   69
Bampton, Rose   40
Barber, Samuel   44
Barlow, Howard   40 54
Basie, Count   42
Beach, Mrs. H. H. A.   45

Belafonte, Harry   56
Bellamann, Henry   42 45
Bennett, Robert Russell   42 62
Bennett, Tony   65
Berigan, Bunny   42
Berlin, Irving   42 63
Bernstein, Leonard   44 60
Biggs, E. Power   50
Blitzstein, Marc   40 64
Bloch, Ernest   53 59
Boone, Pat   59
Boulanger, Nadia   62
Boulez, Pierre   69
Brice, Fanny   46 51
Brubeck, Dave   56

Cage, John   61
Callas, Maria   56
Calloway, Cab   45
Campbell, Glen   69
Cantor, Eddie   41 54 65
Carmichael, Hoagy   41

Hines, Earl   67
Hines, Jerome   63
Hirt, Al   67
Horne, Lena   44
Horne, Marilyn   67
Hovhaness, Alan   65
Hurok, Sol   41   56
Hutton, Betty   50

Ives, Burl   46   60
Ives, Charles   47   54

Jackson, Mahalia   57
Janis, Byron   66
Johnson, Edward   43   59
Johnson, Hall   45   70
Jolson, Al   40   50
Jones, LeRoi   70
Joplin, Janis   70

Kahn, Gus   41
Kapell, William   48   54
Kay, Beatrice   42
Kelley, Edgar Stillman   45
Kern, Jerome   42   45
Kirchner, Leon   67
Kirsten, Dorothy   48
Kitt, Eartha   55
Kolodin, Irving   47
Korngold, Erich Wolfgang   43   58
Koussevitsky, Serge   40   51
Kreisler, Fritz   62
Krupa, Gene   47
Kyser, Kay   41

Laine, Frankie   56
Lane, Burton   67
Latouche, John   40   56
Lawrence, Carol   61
Lawrence, Steve   64
Layton, Joe   70
Lee, Peggy   63
Leinsdorf, Erich   63
Lennon, John   65
Lerner, Alan Jay,
   and Frederick Loewe   58
Lev, Ray   49   68
Levant, Oscar   40   52
Lewis, John   62
Lhevinne, Rosina   61
Liberace   54
Loesser, Frank   45   69
Lombardo, Guy   46

Maazel, Lorin   65
Martin, Mary   44
Mathis, Johnny   65
Maynor, Dorothy   40   51
McKuen, Rod   70
Mehta, Zubin   69
Mellers, Wilfrid   62
Melton, James   45   61
Mennin, Peter   64
Menotti, Gian-Carlo   47
Mercer, Johnny   48
Merman, Ethel   41
Merrill, Robert   52
Miller, Glenn   42
Milnes, Sherrill   70
Minnelli, Liza   70
Mitropoulos, Dimitri   41   61
Monk, Thelonious   64

Monroe, Vaughn   42
Moore, Grace   44   47
Morath, Max   63
Mulligan, Gerry   60
Munsel, Patrice   45

Newman, Alfred   43   70
Nikolais, Alwin   68
Niles, John Jacob   59

Oberlin, Russell   60
Odell, George   44   49
Odetta   60
O'Horgan, Tom   70
Ozawa, Seiji   68

Page, Patti   65
Partch, Harry   65
Peters, Roberta   54
Piston, Walter   61
Porter, Cole   40   64
Powers, Marie   51
Presley, Elvis   59
Price, Leontyne   61

Raskin, Judith   64
Robbins, Jerome   47
Robeson, Paul   41
Rodgers, Richard   40   51
Romberg, Sigmund   45   51
Rome, Harold   42
Rorem, Ned   67
Rose, Billy   40   66
Rudel, Julius   65

Sainte-Marie, Buffy   69
Sandburg, Carl   40   67
Schillinger, Joseph   43
Schippers, Thomas   70
Schuller, Gunther   64
Schuman, William   42   62
Scott, Hazel   43
Shankar, Ravi   68
Shaw, Artie   41
Shaw, Robert   68
Shore, Dinah   42   66
Sills, Beverly   69
Simone, Nina   68
Sinatra, Frank   43   60
Skilton, Charles Sanford   41
Slonimsky, Nicolas   55
Smith, Carleton Sprague   60
Smith, Kate   40   65
Spaeth, Sigmund   42   66
Spitalny, Phil   40   70
Starr, Ringo   65
Steber, Eleanor   43
Stein, Gertrude   46
Steiner, Max   43
Still, William Grant   41
Stoessel, Albert   43
Stokowski, Leopold   41   53
Streisand, Barbra   64
Suesse, Dana   40
Swarthout, Gladys   44   69

Taylor, Deems   40   66
Templeton, Alec   40   63
Thebom, Blanche   48
Thomas, Jess   64
Thomas, John Charles   43   61
Thomson, Virgil   40
Tibbett, Lawrence   45   60

4   **DICHTER, HARRY, and ELLIOTT SHAPIRO   Early American Sheet Music; Its Lure And Its Lore, 1768-1889**   Including a Directory of Early American Music Publishers New York: Bowker, 1941   xxvii, 287p   foreword   intro   "Lithographers and Artists Working on American Sheet Music Before 1870" p 249-57   illus   index

Here, two of the grand old men of American sheet-music collecting (Dichter a dealer, Shapiro a collector) parade their "high spots" (collectors' slang for choice and famous items). As opposed to practices in the larger library sheet-music collections, private collectors arrange their material by subject matter; hence, Dichter and Shapiro have arranged their bibliography in this manner. There are sections on presidential music, the Civil War, transportation, etc. The index helps locate a title if you cannot guess its subject classification.

I have seldom found inaccurate data in this book. Even if highly selective, it is a fine and indispensable tool. Incidentally, the "lore" of the subtitle is covered to a certain degree, but I'm not sure about the "lure." Can a bibliography transmit any particular "allurement" of a subject? I guess it depends on how susceptible one is to being lured.

5   **Dictionary of American Biography**   Editors: vols. 1-3 Allen Johnson; vols. 4-7 Allen Johnson and Dumas Malone; vols. 8-20 Dumas Malone; Supplement 1 Harris E. Starr; Supplement 2 Robert L. Schuyler and Edward T. James   Published under the auspices of the American Council of Learned Societies   New York: Charles Scribner's Sons; London: Milford, 1928-37; Supplements, 1944, 1958   20 vols   (*R* Scribner's, 1943, 21 vols.; 1946, 11 vols.)

This is the major scholarly general dictionary containing biographies of those "who have made some significant contribution to American life in its manifold aspects"—(introduction to vol. 1, p v). The most prominent names are here, as well as some who, "by the caprice of fortune, have been lost from view"—(p vi). No one alive after 1940 is included. The biographies are generally substantial (if not entirely infallible), are based on original source material, and include bibliographies.

The **DAB**'s coverage of figures in American music is uneven. Certain omissions are inexplicable; on the other hand, quite a number of persons are included whose "significant contribution to American life" is questionable. Certain composer-biographees have not enjoyed posthumous fame, a situation due not entirely to "the caprice of fortune." Nevertheless, many of the articles are very fine and should not be overlooked as a prime source of both biographical and bibliographical data.

There is no index within the **DAB** itself. In 1937 Scribner's issued a separate index which is now apparently rare and not to be found in many libraries. One section of the index is an arrangement of persons in the dictionary by occupation. In searching for music figures here, one must look under various headings: Composer, Conductor, Cantor, Organist, Singer, Minstrel, Songwriter, Music Publisher, etc. It is difficult to predict who will be where. My favorite category is simply Musician, under which will be found John Hill Hewitt and Victor Herbert, among other composers (but James Hewitt and Reginald De Koven are listed under the Composer heading). Creative indexing at its best!

Because the index is not widely available, I give here a comprehensive list of composers represented in the **DAB**; "S1" or "S2" following a composer's name means that an article about him appears in one or the other supplement.

Allen, Nathan H.

Baker, Benjamin
Bartlett, Homer
Beck, Johann Heinrich
Billings, William
Bird, Arthur
Blodgett, Benjamin
Bristow, George F.
Buck, Dudley
Burton, Frederick

Carr, Benjamin
Chadwick, George W.   (S2)
Coerne, Louis Adolphe
Converse, Charles C.
Converse, Frederick S.   (S1)

Damrosch, Leopold
De Koven, Reginald
Dresel, Otto
Dunham, Henry

Edwards, Julian
Eichberg, Julius
Emery, Stephen
Emmett, Daniel

Fairlamb, James R.
Foote, Arthur   (S1)
Foster, Stephen
Fry, William Henry

Ganss, Henry
Gershwin, George   (S1)
Gilbert, Henry F.
Gilchrist, William
Gleason, Frederic Grant

Godowsky, Leopold   (S1)
Goldbeck, Robert
Goldmark, Rubin   (S1)
Gottschalk, Louis Moreau
Griffes, Charles T.

Hadley, Henry   (S1)
Hammerstein, Oscar
Harney, Benjamin ("Ben")   (S1)
Harris, Charles K.
Hastings, Thomas
Hays, William
Heinrich, Antony Philip
Hemmeter, John
Herbert, Victor
Hewitt, James
Hewitt, John Hill
Hoffman, Richard
Holden, Oliver
Holyoke, Samuel
Hopkinson, Francis
Humiston, William Henry

Jackson, George K.
Johns, Clayton   (S2)

Kaiser, Alois
Keller, Mathias
Klein, Bruno
Koemmenich, Louis
Kroeger, Ernest R.   (S2)

Lang, Benjamin
Law, Andrew
Liebling, Emil
Loeffler, Charles Martin   (S2)
Lutkin, Peter

MacDowell, Edward
Maretzek, Max
Marzo, Eduardo
Mason, William
Mitchell, Nahum
Musin, Ovide

Nevin, Ethelbert
Nevin, George
Nuno, Jaime

Ochmler, Leo
Oliver, Joseph ("King")   (S1)
Osgood, George

Paine, John Knowles
Palmer, Horatio R.
Parker, Horatio W.
Parker, James
Pease, Alfred
Perabo, Johann
Phillips, Philip
Pratt, Silas

Reinagle, Alexander
Ritter, Frédéric Louis
Rogers, Clara
Root, Frederic Woodman
Root, George Frederick
Rosenblatt, Joseph
Runcie, Constance
Rybner, Martin

Sandler, Jacob
Schelling, Ernest   (S1)
Schindler, Kurt   (S2)
Scott, John
Selby, William

Shaw, Oliver
Sherwood, William
Sobolewski, J. Friedrich
Sousa, John Philip
Southard, Lucien H.
Spicker, Max
Stanley, Albert
Stark, Edward
Sternberg, Constantin Edler Von
Stewart, Humphrey
Swan, Timothy

Taylor, Raynor
Thayer, Whitney
Tobani, Theodore
Trajetta, Philip
Tuckey, William

Van Der Stucken, Frank Valentin
Vogrich, Max

Warren, Richard Henry
Warren, Samuel
Webb, George J.
Weidig, Adolf
Weld, Arthur
Whiting, Arthur   (S1)
Whiting, George
Wight, Frederick
Wilson, Mortimer
Wolle, John
Woodbury, I. B.
Woolf, Benjamin
Work, Henry Clay

Zach, Max
Zeuner, Charles

6   **EAGON, ANGELO**   **Catalog of Published Concert Music by American Composers**
2nd ed. Metuchen, N.J.: The Scarecrow Press, 1969   viii, 348p   foreword   indices (authors; composers) (reviewed *Notes* 26:759-60 June 1970)

A reasonably comprehensive catalog of concert music "generally available in some
printed form for purchase."

Titles are arranged under the following headings: Voice (solo, chorus, etc.); Instrumental (solo and ensembles); Concert Jazz; Percussion; Orchestra; Opera; Band. The
information given for each title is adequate (inclusion of publication dates would
have been helpful, however); individual timings are included in several categories. A
useful book.

7   **FULD, JAMES J.**   **The Book of World-Famous Music; Classical, Popular and Folk**
Foreword by William Lichtenwanger   Rev. and enl. ed. New York: Crown, 1971
xiii, 688p preface intro index

The main purpose of this book is to describe and locate (in libraries and private collections) the first printed editions of hundreds of pieces designated by Fuld as
"world famous." Much American popular and folk music is included. Fuld gives
brief biographical sketches of some composers and quite detailed background information on the history and evaluation of certain songs (e.g. "We Shall Overcome" and
"Battle Hymn of the Republic"). An incipit is included for each composition. Splendid detective work. Delightful reading.

8   **Grove's Dictionary of Music and Musicians** [2nd ed., 1904-10] **American Supplement** Being the sixth volume of the complete work   Waldo Selden Pratt, ed.;
Charles N. Boyd, associate ed. New York: The Macmillan Co., 1920   vii, 412p
preface photos (*R* Philadelphia: Theodore Presser, 1920, under the title *American Music and Musicians*)

—————————————————. [3rd ed., 1927-35] **American Supplement** . . .
New ed. with new material c1928 . . . vii, 438p preface photos "Appendix,
1928" p413-38

This American stepchild of great *Grove's* seems now terribly stately, humorless, and a bit faded (though perhaps less so than its famous parent). Unquestionably, however, it filled an urgent need in 1920 and 1928 and may still be considered a generally fine work. Pratt seems to have done his work well—if with small relish: the tone of his prefatory remarks in both editions is somewhat fretful and apologetic.

Not all American musicians of note will be found in the **Supplement** but rather in the dictionary proper. Some are in both; e.g. the major MacDowell article, with photo, is in the dictionary, with additional information in the **Supplement**. A unique (but not necessarily fine) feature of the **Supplement** is the so-called "Chronological Register." This is divided into five rather arbitrary sections covering the colonial era to 1920, with a brief essay on each period and an alphabetical listing of the musicians who worked during it; there are cross-references to articles in both the dictionary and **Supplement**.

I will not comment on *Grove's'* American coverage in any of its editions (including the 5th). Certain inadequacies in this area have long been noted (check Eric Blom's Gershwin article, for instance, and make your own notes). The forthcoming 6th edition has high promise of rectifying all this.

9   **HIXON, DONALD L.   Music in Early America: A Bibliography of Music in Evans**
Metuchen, N.J.: The Scarecrow Press, 1970   xv, 607p   intro   indices

The "Evans" of the subtitle is a familiar allusion to Charles Evans's classic and monumental work *American Bibliography; a chronological dictionary of all books, pamphlets and periodical publications printed in the United States of America from the genesis of printing in 1639 down to and including the year 1800* (Chicago: printed for the author, 1903-59; 14 vols. R New York: Peter Smith, 1941.   13 vols. + indices). Hixon's bibliography also draws upon the Readex Corporation's microprint edition *Early American Imprints, 1639-1800* (Clifford K. Shipton, ed., New York, 1955-), which aims to reproduce every item listed in Evans.

This work extracts from *Evans* all items containing printed musical notation, whether in separate sheet-music form or in collections, books, pamphlets, and broadsides. The musical content of periodicals, newspapers, and most other serial publications has not been indexed. The book is in six parts:

    1) Alphabetical composer-editor-compiler arrangement of all items currently

available in the Readex *Early American Imprints* microprint edition. Contents of all secular collections are listed;

    2) Alphabetical composer-editor-compiler arrangement of items from *Evans* not in the Readex edition at the time of writing;

    3) Biographical sketches of composers;

    4) Composer-title index;

    5) Title-composer index;

    6) Index of *Evans* serial numbers.

Since this work as a whole is an index to the music in *Evans*, the author has omitted descriptive elements for each title that are included in the parent work. He has also omitted the library locations for each title. Thus, while Hixon's book is admirable and useful in many ways on its own, for maximum utility it must be used with the original Evans bibliography at hand. This fact will surely be lamented by all who are seeking detailed information on early American music imprints but who do not have easy access to the Evans work or to the Readex *Early American Imprints* microprint edition (it retails for $8000).

For student use the Hixon book will not replace **Sonneck-Upton (12)** as the most convenient and substantial guide to pre-1800 music imprints, nor was it intended to do so. The unique features of the two books, however, are complementary: **Sonneck-Upton** has the detail lacking in **Hixon**; **Hixon** includes sacred music whereas **Sonneck-Upton** includes only those sacred collections that contain some secular pieces. Anyone investigating this field would do well to use these two fine works in tandem.

10 JONES, F. O. Handbook of American Music and Musicians, Containing Biographies of American Musicians, and Histories of the Principal Institutions, Firms and Societies
Canaseraga, N.Y.: Pub. by F. O. Jones, 1886   182p   preface   (*R* Da Capo Press)

————————————————. New ed. Buffalo: C. W. Moulton, 1887.

This charming miniature encyclopedia is not infallible but it is still quite useful for identifying composers, singers, and other performers of the period. Entries also include musical titles such as cantatas, oratorios, songs, hymn and psalm collections, as well as musical organizations.

The content of the "new edition" is identical with that of the 1886 edition; it should be regarded as a second printing with a new imprint.

11 MATTFELD, JULIUS, compiler **Variety Music Cavalcade, 1620-1950** A Chronology of Vocal and Instrumental Music Popular in the United States With an introduction by Abel Green New York: Prentice-Hall, 1952 xvi, 637p preface "List of Publishers" p633-37 index (of song titles)

_____. **Variety Music Cavalcade, 1620-1961** Rev. ed. Englewood Cliffs, N.J.: Prentice-Hall, 1962 xxiii, 713p (reviewed _Notes_ 20:33-4 Spring 1963)

_____. **Variety Music Cavalcade, 1620-1969** Third ed. 1971 xx, 766p appendix ("Some Late-Blooming Perennials" p711-14)

Ostensibly a compilation of the best-known popular songs and instrumental pieces in the U.S., listed by year (how Mattfeld determined which were the hit pieces among the first colonists is somewhat vague). The book is much more, however: almanac, factbook, and general source of Americana relating to politics, literature, science, economics, music, show business, crime, sports, and national disasters. A wild and wonderful book.

The lists (rather stingy ones) and "historical notes" for 1962-71 in the third edition were prepared by Herm Schoenfeld. The appendix in this edition is a chronological list of well-known pieces overlooked in the earlier editions. The useful list of publishers was dropped after the first edition.

I once expressed disappointment to the amazing Mr. Mattfeld (1893-1968) that only music titles had been indexed. He was surprised: what reason could there be for using his book other than locating titles? There was an obvious retort to the question but I let it pass.

12 SONNECK, O. G. **Bibliography of Early Secular American Music** Washington, D.C.: Printed for the author by H. L. McQueen, 1905 194p preface index

_____. **A Bibliography of Early Secular American Music (18th Century)**, by Oscar George Theodore Sonneck Rev. and enlarged by William Treat Upton Washington D.C.: The Library of Congress, Music Division, 1945 xvi, 616p prefaces index (_R_ Da Capo Press, 1964 With a preface by Irving Lowens.) (reviewed _Inter-American Institute for Musical Research Yearbook_ 1:134 1965)

In his preface to the first edition (a run of 200 copies paid for by the compiler himself), Sonneck stated:

I have aimed at a complete collection of titles of secular music and books, pamphlets, essays, etc., relating to secular music —

1. Issued by the American press prior to the nineteenth century and extant in certain libraries to be mentioned;
2. Issued but not extant in these libraries;
3. Written by native or naturalized Americans and extant in manuscript;
4. Written by the same but apparently neither published nor extant.

This was a tremendous accomplishment, especially at a time when work in this field was all but non-existent. Upton's revision of Sonneck's classic took three years; it multiplied by several times the size of the original. Upton also rearranged and enlarged upon certain of Sonneck's original material and produced these new features: list of articles and essays relating to music; list of composers (with biographical sketches); list of songsters; list of first lines; list of American patriotic music; list of opera librettos; list of publishers, printers, and engravers.

The bibliography proper is arranged by title with full descriptions, annotations, and library locations.

13 WOLFE, RICHARD J. Secular Music in America, 1801-1825; A Bibliography
Introduction by Carleton Sprague Smith   New York: The New York Public Library, 1964   3 vols.   1238p   preface   illus   appendix   indices   (reviewed *Notes* 21:356-7 Summer 1964)

A monumental set containing data on all U.S. secular music imprints (over 10,000), published during the years specified, that could be located in libraries and private collections. Begins where **Sonneck-Upton (12)** ends. Meticulous scholarship. Highest quality.

Unlike the **Sonneck-Upton** title arrangement, the pieces in **Wolfe** are grouped by composer; anonymous pieces are, however, listed by title within the alphabetical sequence. **Wolfe** should not be overlooked as a source of biographical information; sketches for the lesser-known composers are derived largely from painstaking original research.

Special features: The appendix lists 18th-century imprints located since the publication of **Sonneck-Upton**, redated imprints, and additional copies of 18th-century imprints already listed in **Sonneck-Upton**; and there are five elaborate indexes (titles; first lines; publishers, engravers, and printers; publishers' plate and publication numbering systems; general index).

II

HISTORICAL STUDIES

14 CHASE, GILBERT   America's Music; From the Pilgrims to the present   New York: McGraw-Hill, 1955   xxiii, 733p

_____.   Rev. 2nd ed., 1966   xxi, 759p   Preface to the 2nd ed.   Foreword (by Douglas Moore)   intro   "A note on recordings" p693-95   bibliography   index   "About the author" p[761]   (reviewed *Notes* 23:741 June 1967)

I quote from my review (of the second edition) which appeared in *American Choral Review* (Spring 1967):

> Since its first appearance, the Chase book has become the standard history of music in this country. It was the first general history of American music to give major consideration to popular-vernacular forms and to declare that these forms were quite as worthy of study as art music. Today this belief is widely accepted and one suspects that Chase's book is to a considerable degree responsible. No other work of its kind is as inclusive, as broad-minded, and as persuasive. . . .

> . . . close to half of the new edition represents either completely new material or revised material. The most conspicuous, and the most valuable, of the new material is contained in the final chapter. Entitled "The Scene in the Sixties," this 36-page section presents an excellent sampling of the latest currents in American music. Composers from the East Coast, the West Coast, and a few places in between, are represented; selected works are discussed, biographical details, and, most importantly, statements of the composers' aesthetic positions are included.

> Further new material has been added to the book. A new section on recordings has been incorporated and the bibliography has been enlarged. The career of every living composer covered has been brought up to date; a number of composers who have come to some prominence since the first edition are now included. Several chapters, such as those on jazz, opera, and musical comedy, have

been re-written, former material being compressed, rearranged, or (unfortunately) omitted altogether, presumably to make room for the new material. The chapter on Indian tribal music, one of the least pertinent to the study, has been dropped. Because of these deletions, many who have the first edition will want to hold on to it.

15 **ELSON, LOUIS C. The History of American Music** With twelve full-page photogravures and one hundred and two illustrations in the text New York: The Macmillan Co., 1904 xiii, 380p (Series: *The History of American Art*, vol. 2) (*R* Burt Franklin)

────────────────────────. With . . . one hundred and three illustrations in the text Rev. ed. 1915 xiii, 387p "Supplementary Chapter" p367-72 bibliography indices

────────────────────────. With . . . one hundred and six illustrations in the text Rev. to 1925 by Arthur Elson 1925 xiii, 423p "Supplementary Chapters to 1925" p373-404 bibliography indices

Writing just 21 years after the appearance of Frédéric Ritter's pioneer book **(22)**, Elson was bold enough to regard his own work as "the" history of American music. Foolhardy, to be sure, but of great interest. Elson had developed a certain perspective of the work of Ritter, seeing it more or less for what it was. After praising the immigrant Ritter for his cultural missionary work in Cincinnati and New York, and for his various literary efforts, Elson states that "another volume on music in America had less of success, for Dr. Ritter approached his subject with little sympathy. . . . of the American composers he had not a word to say. . . . he was among us, but not of us"–(p336-37).

Elson had considerable sophistication; he was also a proper Bostonian. His book reflects this mix: many of his ideas are striking, but his tone is generally somber and conventional. He provides considerable information on composers active at the time, and a chapter on national and patriotic music; he also includes a strange discussion of folk music dealing largely with Stephen Foster (!). Much of the biographical information is still useful. Quite magnificent plates on quality paper (in the original editions).

Note on the reprint edition: Why was the first rather than the last edition reprinted?

The strongest reason would seem to be that at the time of reprinting, the first edition was the only one in the public domain, hence no fees had to be paid. Oh, well. . . .

16   FARWELL, ARTHUR, and W. DERMOT DARBY, editors   Music in America
Introduction by Arthur Farwell   New York: The National Society of Music, 1915
xxix, 478p   photos   bibliography   index   (Series: *The Art of Music; A Comprehensive Library of Information for Music Lovers and Musicians*)

The 14-volume *The Art of Music*, of which the Farwell-Darby study is vol. 4, is an unorthodox encyclopedia full of little surprises. Among its components are a "narrative history" of music in three volumes, a volume on orchestral writing with an introduction by Richard Strauss, a volume on dance with introduction by Anna Pavlova, and two volumes of music selected by Henry Gilbert (with a liberal sample of American pieces, to be sure).

Music in America is a patch-work of material by six writers. Not surprisingly, it is uneven. Certain sections, however, are of high quality: imaginative, original, and buttressed with sound factual information. There are 15 chapters, each signed with initials. I am unaware of the identity of "M.M.M." and "J.S.," authors of single chapters, but "B.L." (two chapters) is apparently Benjamin Lambord and "C.S." (one chapter) César Saerchinger, both associated with the series. The largest contributor, with seven chapters, was the co-editor William Dermot Darby (1885-1947). I would like to know more about Darby, an Irish textile specialist and propagandist for his country's independence, who immigrated to the United States only five years before he worked on the encyclopedia. His chapters on early music in America and other topics are written with unexpected authority and wit. (For more on Darby, see his obituary in *The New York Times*, October 21, 1947.)

The chief distinction of the work is the presence of Arthur Farwell. His introduction and two chapters, "Romanticists and Neo-Romanticists" and "Nationalists, Eclectics and Ultra-Moderns," which together survey the work of over 40 composers, should be essential to any bibliography representative of the best writings in the field. His critical treatment of the composers, both friends and foes, is incisive but never destructive, realistic but always gentle. The introduction is perhaps Farwell's best short essay. It contains a deft description of the book as a study of "appreciation, creation, and administration" (which he terms the major aspects of the history of music in America "in its largest outlines"), and it also provides a brilliant summation of the state of music as he saw it in 1914.

17   HITCHCOCK, H. WILEY   Music in the United States: A Historical Introduction
Englewood Cliffs, N.J.: Prentice-Hall, 1969   270p   bibliographical notes at the ends of chapters   index   (Series: *Prentice-Hall History of Music*)   (reviewed *Music Educators Journal* 57:75 Nov 1970)

This is an excellent, compact survey using what I suppose may now be called the "traditional" approach to the subject (i.e., roughly chronological from the New England colonies to the present). It is also a generous source of annotated bibliography. Hitchcock provides knowing comments on books and articles at the ends of chapters and in footnotes. Though biographical information is necessarily succinct, there are bits on a few figures otherwise difficult to locate (e.g., Charles Grobe, p68-71).

18   HOWARD, JOHN TASKER   Our American Music; Three Hundred Years of it
New York: T.Y. Crowell Co., 1931   xxiii, 713p

_____. **Our American Music; A Comprehensive History from 1620 to the Present**   4th ed. New York: Thomas Y. Crowell Co., 1965   xxii, 944p   preface (1st ed.)   preface to 3rd ed. (1946)   preface to 4th ed.   intro plates   photos   bibliography   index   (reviewed *Music Journal* 24:95 Feb 1966; *American Choral Review* 8:17 n3 1966)

One of the classic histories of the subject. Howard (1890-1964) was a dedicated and accomplished scholar who served American music in numerous ways. Some of his ideas and procedures may seem old-fashioned; no matter, the book contains a great wealth of practical information—extensive biographical coverage, lists of works, good plates. Through four editions over a 34-year span, the book was considerably updated, corrected, and otherwise enlarged. The bibliography for the 4th edition, revised by Karl Kroeger at Howard's request, is one of the very best available.

19   HUGHES, RUPERT   Contemporary American Composers   Being a study of the music of this country, its present conditions and its future, with critical estimates and biographies of the principal living composers; and an abundance of portraits, fac-simile musical autographs, and compositions   Boston: L. C. Page, 1900   xiv, 456p

_____. **American Composers**   A study of the music of this country, and of its future, with biographies of the leading composers of the present time   Being a new revised edition of *Contemporary American Composers*   With

additional chapters by Arthur Elson   Boston: Page Co., 1914   xxii, 582p   foreword
photos   index

An enlightened contemporary view of the later 19th-century American composers by
a distinguished writer. Hughes personally contacted dozens of living composers and
performers; he also examined hundreds of scores. His analytic comments are lively
and imaginative, but he does tend to overrate everything. Information on many little-
known figures. Very good plates.

The second edition is the more desirable because of Elson's added material. A fine
work.

How amazing it is to read both Hughes and Elson on their younger contemporary
Margaret Ruthven Lang and to see her lovely youthful photograph. As I write this
she is living in Boston and, at age 104, is the oldest living American composer—perhaps
the oldest living composer anywhere.

20   **LOWENS, IRVING   Music and Musicians in Early America**   New York: W. W.
Norton, 1964   328p   preface   illus   appendices   index   (reviewed *Journal of
Research in Music Education* 13:60-61 Spring 1965)

These fine articles and papers by one of the distinguished scholars in American music
appeared originally in various books and journals; they were, however, substantially
corrected, amplified, and altered in other ways for this collection. Though there are
valuable bibliographical footnotes throughout, the section titled "Men" contains the
material perhaps most pertinent to this bibliography. Six pieces are devoted to the
personal and professional lives of important earlier figures, namely Daniel Read, the
Edson family, James Hewitt, Heinrich, Fry, and Gottschalk.

The appendix that interests me most is "A Check-list of Writings About Music in the
Periodicals of American Transcendentalism (1835-50)."

21   **MATTHEWS, W. S. B.   A Hundred Years Of Music In America. An Account Of
Musical Effort In America . . .**   Chicago: G. L. Howe, 1889   ix, 715p   intro
photos   "Supplementary Dictionary of American Musicians" p703-15   (*R* AMS
Press)

A generally fine and interesting work. Matthews provides information on numerous
musical organizations, composers, and performers, many of them now obscure. There
are factual errors in the book, but its ambitious scope and over-all accomplishment are
still impressive. The 240 plates are a treasure.

The point-of-view of New Hampshire-born Matthews seems less prejudiced than that of his contemporary Frédéric Ritter (22), though they shared a "things-are-getting-better-all-the-time" philosophy of history.

22　**RITTER, FREDERIC**　**Music In America**　New York: Charles Scribner's Sons, 1883　xiv, 423p　preface　index　(R Burt Franklin)

_____. New ed., with additions, 1890　xiv, 521p (R Johnson Reprint)

The first attempt at a comprehensive history of music in this country. Ritter was an Alsatian musician who came to the U.S.A. in 1856, lived in Cincinnati and New York, and eventually taught at Vassar. Though he was well-meaning, his book is everywhere informed with the undoubtedly typical attitudes toward its subject of the upper-middle class academician of the later 19th century: it is urban-oriented; it venerates the imitation of Old World culture and the new musical establishment; it is defensive. Fascinating as a document of its time and place.

Some practical aspects: despite a liberal smattering of factual errors, the biographical sketches of both well-known and obscure contemporary figures are of interest; there is also a large amount of material on musical organizations.

23　**SONNECK, O. G.**　**Early Concert-Life in America (1731-1800)**　Leipzig: Breitkopf & Härtel, 1907　338p　preface　intro　index　(R Musurgia Publishers, 1949)

Sonneck states in his preface that "biographical and bibliographical data were included in so far only as they seemed called for or affected the biographical notes given in the index to my Bibliography of Early Secular American Music (12)." Nevertheless, there are interesting biographical bits scattered throughout the book, and extensive bibliographical footnotes.

The preface is the source of one of Sonneck's most endearing remarks. Referring indirectly to the pioneer status of his work, he asks critics to forgive his lack of literary brilliancy and "to remember how very difficult a task it is to turn a virgin-forest into a garden."

The fact that this classic study has a Leipzig imprint is more than an irony: it is a damning footnote in the lugubrious history of resistance to the idea of an authentic American musical heritage. No American book publisher in 1907 was interested in Sonneck's manuscript.

III

REGIONAL STUDIES

24 **EDWARDS, GEORGE THORNTON**   **Music and Musicians of Maine**   Being a History of the Progress of Music in the territory which has come to be known as the State of Maine from 1604 to 1928   Portland, Me.: The Southworth Press, 1928   xxv, 542p preface   photos   plates   indices (biographical; general)   (*R* AMS Press)

Edwards begins his book with a prologue devoted to music of the Penobscot and Passamaquoddy Indian tribes and other early music; proceeds with six chapters, each devoted to a specific number of years; and concludes with a biographical dictionary of Maine musicians active at the time of writing.

This is a first-rate study. The biographical information throughout is generous and carefully researched. The photos and plates are rare and marvelous.

25 **GERSON, ROBERT A.**   **Music in Philadelphia**   A history of Philadelphia music, a summary of its current state, and a comprehensive index dictionary   Philadelphia: Theodore Presser, 1940   viii, 422p   preface   photos   plates   index   bibliography (*R* Greenwood Press)

The biographical information here on Benjamin Carr, James Lyon, Francis Hopkinson, and many others is fairly sketchy; however, the brief coverage of many lesser-known figures is valuable. Societies, schools, publishers, and performers are adequately accounted for, but in no depth. The index is good and the bibliography (including unpublished material) is interesting. The title-page's "index dictionary" refers to an A-Z listing at the back of the book that is a regular index interspersed with brief biographical sketches of certain people not dealt with in the text; a rather awkward affair, actually.

26   JOHNSON, H. EARLE   Musical Interludes in Boston, 1795-1830   New York:
Columbia University Press, 1943   xv, 366p   foreword (by Otto Kinkeldey)   preface
plates   appendices   index   (*R* AMS Press)

One of the standard works on earlier Boston music life. Johnson explains the absence
of a bibliography in this way: "The chief source of all research has been the newspapers. . . . other histories, recollections, or compilations are in such varying measure
untrustworthy that it has seemed wiser to record the source materials as they occur by
copious footnotes rather than to perpetuate a bibliography of doubtful value"—
(preface).

There are major accounts of two music-publishing families—the Von Hagens and the
Graupners—and the fascinating organist-composer Dr. George K. Jackson.

The five excellent appendices are:
- list of Von Hagen publications;
- leading vocalists appearing in Boston;
- list of Graupner publications;
- works issued by lesser Boston publishers;
- copyrighted music collections (1791-1827).

27   KNIPPERS, OTTIS J.   Who's Who Among Southern Singers and Composers
Lawrenceberg, Tenn.: James D. Vaughan, 1937   168p   preface   photos   indices
(names; song titles)

Biographies and photos of white gospel-song composers and singers, most all of them
known only regionally. Many were leaders in singing schools. The title index is selective.

28   OSBURN, MARY HUBBELL   Ohio Composers and Musical Authors   Columbus,
O.: Privately published, 1942   238p   intro   "Development of Music in Ohio"
p7-14   bibliography (both with the entries and in the section "References" on p231)
index (to composers)

The author states that her research for this biographical dictionary "has continued
over many years, gathered from personal letters and interviews, and from all possible

written sources"—(p5). The book covers authors, composers, and musicians who were either born in Ohio or lived and worked there. Some articles are obviously sketchy but others are substantial and seem carefully done. Deals with such diverse figures as William Doane (hymn-writer), Benjamin Russell Hanby (famous for "My Darling Nelly Gray"), Tell Taylor ("Down By the Old Mill Stream"), Harry Lawrence Freeman (early black opera composer), David Stanley Smith, Arthur Shepherd, Arne Oldberg, and Beryl Rubinstein. Includes lists of works.

29 UNITED STATES. WORKS PROJECTS ADMINISTRATION. CALIFORNIA
History of Music in San Francisco Series   Edited by Cornel Lengyel   San Francisco
[Reproduced from typescript]   (*R* AMS Press)

> Vol. 1   *Music of the Gold Rush Era* (1939)
> Vol. 2   *A San Francisco Songster, 1849-1939* (1939)
> Vol. 3   *The Letters of Miska Hauser, 1853* (1939)
> Vol. 4   *Celebrities in El Dorado, 1850-1906* (1940)
> Vol. 5   *Fifty Local Prodigies* (1940)
> Vol. 6   *Early Master Teachers* (1940)
> Vol. 7   *An Anthology of Music Criticism* (1942)

This work is one of the few monuments in the literature of United States music. It is a product of the Works Projects Administration, the government-sponsored agency of the 1930s that provided jobs for musicians and writers, among others, who found themselves with little money and lots of spare time.

The set is a compendium of early San Francisco music and musical life. The biographical information is abundant; much of it cannot be found in any other source. In the original edition there are actual prints of numerous rare photos pasted in throughout the set. Each volume contains its own bibliography, appendices, and index.

IV

TOPICAL STUDIES

Folk Music (including Country-and-Western)

30 **Check-list of recorded songs in the English language in the Archive of American Folk Song to July, 1940**   Alphabetical list with geographical index   Washington, D.C.: The Library of Congress, 1942   (*R* Arno Press)

[vol. 1] *A-K*   p1-216   Foreword (by Harold Spivacke)   intro
[vol. 2] *L-Z*   p217-456
[vol. 3] *Geographical Index*   138p

This huge check-list can be a valuable asset to anyone working in the American folk field, especially since recordings of any of the titles may be ordered from the Library of Congress (information on ordering is included in the introduction).

Each title entry contains the following information: "the name of the singer(s) or (and) performer(s), the place and date of the recording, the name of the collector(s) and the call number of the disc"—(introduction). All titles appear again in the *Geographical Index* under the proper state and county of origin.

31 **Folk Music: A Catalog of Folk Songs, Ballads, Dances, Instrumental Pieces, and Folk Tales of the United States and Latin America on Phonograph Records**
Catalog of Phonograph Records   Washington, D.C.: Music Division, Recording Laboratory, Reference Department, Library of Congress, 1964   iv, 107p   "The Archive of Folk Song" (by Rae Korson) p iii   introductory note

"This catalog lists 107 discs (78 rpm) containing 341 titles and 59 discs (33-1/3 rpm) with 899 titles. They are representative of the best of more than 16,000 records in the collection of the Archive of Folk Song"—(introductory note).

In three sections: listing by album (available on 78 or 33-1/3) with complete contents and credits; index of album titles; index of titles of individual songs and pieces. All records may be ordered from the Archive (order blanks included).

32 **GENTRY, LINNELL   A History and Encyclopedia of Country, Western, and Gospel Music**   2nd ed. (completely rev.)   Nashville: Clairmont Corp., 1969   xiv, 598p   foreword (by Tex Ritter)   intro

Gentry states that the purpose of the book is to present needed information on the subject through "(1) reprints of 76 significant articles or stories (published 1908-1968) from selected magazines, newspapers, brochures, and other periodicals (1961 edition contained 37 reprints); and (2) over 600 biographies of singers, musicians, comedians, comediennes, and others who have assisted in popularizing country, western, and gospel music in the 20th century (1961 edition included 334 biographies)"—(introduction).

The reprints (mostly brief) are handy but hardly justify the use of the word history in the title. The biographies, which include addresses, are detailed and seem carefully done. The coverage is largely of living performers.

One stunning flaw is the (total?) omission of black gospel performers. Not even Mahalia Jackson, Clara Ward, or Sister Rosetta Tharpe are included. Why? If the word "white" were added to the title, preceding the word "gospel," Gentry's intention would be clear.

33 **HAYWOOD, CHARLES   A Bibliography of North American Folklore and Folksong**
This edition is limited to 1,500 copies, of which 1,493 are for sale   New York: Greenberg, 1951   xxx, 1292p   intro   index   maps

_____. 2nd rev. ed.   New York: Dover Publications, 1961 (reviewed *Notes* 20:67 Winter 1962-63)

    Vol. 1   *The American People North of Mexico, Including Canada*
        xxx, p3-748   preface to the Dover ed   intro
    Vol. 2   *The American Indians North of Mexico, Including the Eskimos*
        ix, p750-1301   index   index supplement ("Composers, Arrangers, Performers") p1293-1301

This masterly authoritative work, certainly basic to any research in American folksong, is mercifully easier to handle in the Dover edition than in the massive one-volume 1st edition. In using the Dover set, however, one must remember that the index (and its supplement) to the whole is in Volume 2.

The books have a rather complex arrangement. Volume 1 contains five major bibliographies which are divided into sections on folklore and folksong. Each section has several subject divisions and subdivisions (general studies, collections, arrangements, recordings, etc.). Volume 2 (on Indians) is in two parts, a general bibliography and a bibliography of individual culture areas. Material in each culture area is broken down under the names of tribes. Here again, there are numerous divisions and subdivisions. In using this rich but complicated work, I find that after locating an item in the index and finding the full citation within a volume, it is helpful to consult the table of contents to get my bearings. Try this out and you will see what I mean.

It should be remembered that no material published after 1951 is cited in the 1961 edition. The latter is essentially a republication (with corrections) of the earlier book; the revisions consist of the separation of the material into two volumes, as mentioned, and the addition of the composer-arranger-performer index. Therefore, for post-1951 coverage one should use **Lawless (34)**. This is particularly important for locating long-playing records, since most references in **Haywood** are to 78-rpm discs.

34   **LAWLESS, RAY M.**   **Folksingers and Folkways in America**   A handbook of biography, bibliography, and discography   Illustrated from paintings by Thomas Hart Benton and others, and from designs in Steuben Glass   New rev. ed. with Special Supplement   New York: Duell, Sloan and Pearce, 1965   xviii, 750p   prefaces (reviewed *Music Educators Journal* 52:107 Nov-Dec 1965)

Pages 3-662 contain the material from the first (1960) edition but incorporate "corrections and suggestions . . . sent in by various scholars." The new material is contained essentially in the Special Supplement beginning on page [663]. Each of the two sections contains its own table of contents, preface, and indices. This is too bad. In searching for a title or other bit of information one must remember to check in two places. Nevertheless, the book is packed with useful data.

Notable features:

- generally brief but good biographical sketches of folksingers;
- section on folk instruments;
- annotated bibliography of folksong collections and "background books";
- check-list of song titles located in collections;
- discographies.

The reproductions of Benton paintings and Steuben designs seem pointless to me in this context.

35 **A List of American Folksongs Currently Available on Records** Compiled by the Archive of American Folksong of the Library of Congress   Washington, D.C.: Library of Congress, 1953   176p   index (of album titles and performers' names)

The records listed are from the Archive's collection as well as those released on commercial labels. The work is an alphabetical list of songs with credits and title of album in which each song is located.

36 **MALONE, BILL C.   Country Music U.S.A.; A Fifty-year History**   Austin and London: The University of Texas Press, for The American Folklore Society, 1968   xii, 422p   preface   photos   bibliography (of materials used)   index   (Publications of The American Folklore Society   *Memoir Series*   General ed., John Greenway   Vol. 54, 1968)   (reviewed *Notes* 26:37-9 Sept 1969)

A magnificent work. Filled with detailed biographical information; excellent bibliographical footnotes. The bibliography of materials used in preparing the book is extremely rich: unpublished letters, interviews, manuscripts, record catalogs, mail-order catalogs, newspapers, recordings, books and pamphlets, theses, dissertations, and articles. Highly recommended.

37 **SHELTON, ROBERT   The Country Music Story; A Picture History of Country and Western Music**   Photos by Burt Goldblatt   Indianapolis . . .: Bobbs-Merrill, 1966   256p   "A Selective List of Country and Western LP Recordings" p238-42   index (of names)   (reviewed *Billboard* 78:6 Dec 17 1966)

The newer photos by Goldblatt and the older ones from numerous sources are evocative, amusing, and touching. A superb visual record with historical commentary. The discography is highly selective but practical.

38 **STAMBLER, IRWIN, and GRELUN LANDON** **Encyclopedia of Folk, Country and Western Music** New York: St. Martin's Press, 1969 viii, 396p photos appendices discography bibliography (reviewed *Saturday Review* 52:50 Dec 6 1969)

Entries under individuals, groups, names of radio programs, festivals, and a few instruments (e.g., dulcimer, sitar). The reportage is breezy but generally sound. Liberal cross-references. Three articles by Sam Hinton, Bill Anderson, and Ed Kahn, as well as the lists of awards in the appendices, enhance a very handy volume.

Black Music as a Genre

39 **CUNEY-HARE, MAUD** **Negro Musicians and Their Music** Washington, D.C.: Associated Publishers, 1936 preface intro (by Clarence Cameron White) illus photos appendix ("African Musical Instruments") bibliography index

There is much useful information here, biographical (especially about the earlier 20th-century generation of composers and performers) and otherwise. The photos are beautiful and the bibliography is interesting (if limited). However, the author is uncomfortable discussing ragtime and jazz, about which she apparently knew little. Negro popular music in general seems to embarrass her and she attempts to rationalize away its more "vulgar" aspects. An air of gentility hangs heavily over the book, and I always become annoyed after reading a few pages.

40 **HEILBUT, TONY** **The Gospel Sound: Good News and Bad Times** New York: Simon and Schuster, 1971 350p intro photos discography indices (names; song titles)

The modish title of Heilbut's book is hardly a fair indication of its considerable substance and originality. It deals with the music, performers, composers, publishers, churches, and life-style bound up in the modern black gospel movement, described as "barely forty years old" though continuing "a tradition of singing, preaching, and shouting familiar to generations of black people"—(introduction). Heilbut's style is casual, even slangy, and given to occasional hyperbole (" . . . Brewster is a magnificent songwriter, at the very least a Milton to Thomas A. Dorsey's Shakespeare" [—p127]); but no matter, the array of little-known biographical and other data, historical perspective, and the generally graceful criticism more than compensate.

The book was apparently fifteen years in the making (see Heilbut's acknowledgments, p326), and it was obviously a labor of great devotion. Fortunately, the majority of key figures in modern gospel were alive and available for interviews during the period of research. The matchless feature of the book is the quantity of excerpts from these interviews, all crackling with earthy wit, vivid, often heartbreaking recollections, truths hard-learned from years of poverty, grueling travels, and dishonest managers and associates. They are transcribed with what seems careful retention of the speakers' occasional dialect patterns.

Heilbut frequently remarks that the recordings of gospel music do not adequately convey the passion of live performances; there is no such problem in this book. The interviews (and Heilbut's narrative) do communicate a passion born of deep convictions and a love for gospel music.

The following individuals and groups receive major treatment:

Anderson, Queen C.	Harris, R. H.
Brewster, Rev. W. Herbert	Jackson, Mahalia
Caesar, Shirley	Jeter, Rev. Claude, and
Campbell, Deloris Barret	The Swan Silvertones
Caravans, The	Martin, Roberta
Cheeks, Rev. Julius, and	Martin, Sallie
The Sensational Nightingales	Pilgrim Travelers, The
Cleveland, James	Smith, Willie Mae Ford
Coates, Dorothy Love, and	Soul Stirrers, The
The Original Gospel Harmonettes	Staple Singers, The
Cooke, Sam	Tharpe, Sister Rosetta
Davis, Ruth	Tucker, Ira, and
Dixon, Jessy	The Dixie Hummingbirds
Dorsey, Thomas A.	Ward, Clara
Griffin, Bessie	Williams, Marion

41 PATTERSON, LINDSAY, compiler and ed.   The Negro in Music and Art   2nd ed. rev. New York: Publishers Company, under the auspices of The Association for the Study of Negro Life and History, 1969   304p   intro   illus   plates   photos   bibliography   index   (Series: *International Library of Negro Life and History*)

One of a ten-volume series, this work is notable largely for its superb photographs and illustrations. It covers a wide range of black music in a series of prose pieces excerpted from earlier books and other sources. Biographical information on composers and performers tends to be sketchy and superficial. The bibliography is limited.

42 SOUTHERN, EILEEN   The Music of Black Americans: A History   New York: W. W. Norton, 1971   xviii, 552p   preface   photos   illus   bibliography and discography (by chapter) p511-32   index   (reviewed *Notes* 28:43-4 Sept 1971)

This is the first comprehensive history of the musical activities of black Americans in the United States. It is a sweeping synthesis filled with much valuable data. Biographical information is abundant: Dr. Southern states in her preface that the chief emphasis of the book "has been placed on the creators of the music, whether they were anonymous slaves of the ante-bellum period, ballad writers of the Gay Nineties, jazzmen of the early twentieth century, or composers of symphonic music." She also discusses "a number of musicians who were primarily performers."

The bibliography is certainly the best for this subject ever assembled.

Because of its general nature, detailed investigation of certain areas had to be slighted. The author acknowledges this fact, stating that "much research yet needs to be done in all areas of musical activities, particularly in the earlier periods. Perhaps the present study will stimulate such general research and investigation into special aspects of black American music"—(preface).

43 TROTTER, JAMES M.   Music and Some Highly Musical People . . .   Boston: Lee and Shepard; New York: Charles T. Dillingham, 1881   353, 152p   preface   illus appendix ("Music" 152p)   (*R* Johnson Reprint)

Trotter (1842-1892) assembled much information on such famous 19th-century black musicians as Elizabeth Taylor Greenfield, Thomas Bethune, Frederick Elliot Lewis, Joseph White, and such groups as The Colored American Opera Company, The Fisk Jubilee Singers, and The Georgia Minstrels. Some of the data is garbled and should be checked against **Southern (42)**, but the book was a considerable achievement for its day and remains impressive.

The appendix contains 13 complete vocal and instrumental pieces.

The lack of an index is a great hindrance. Johnson Reprint Corporation should have prepared one for its 1968 reprint.

Blues, Ragtime, Jazz

44 **BLESH, RUDI, and HARRIET JANIS**   **They All Played Ragtime; The True Story of an American Music**   New York: Alfred A. Knopf, 1950   xviii, 338, xviii p

_____. Rev. and with new additional material . . .   New York: Oak Publications, 1966   xxiv, 347, ix p (reviewed _Down Beat_ 33:42 Nov 17 1966)

_____. New York: Oak Publications; London: Music Sales Limited, 1971   xxiv, 347, ix p   Author's Preface to the Fourth Ed.   intro ("Prelude")   illus   music   photos   "Chronology of Important Ragtime Dates" p273-74   "Lists of Musical Compositions" p275-325   "A List of Player-Piano Rolls" p326-37   "A Selected List of Phonograph Records" p338-47   index

When the subtitle of a book is "the true story of . . ." something, one tends to expect the worst. In this case, however, misgivings are quickly dispelled. The pioneering Blesh·Janis work is a must for its wide range of information on major and minor figures of the ragtime era, although further research in this field will no doubt expand our awareness and set certain details straight, especially concerning Scott Joplin.

The most useful features of the book are the lists of audio materials and the lists of works (I wish these had been indexed; there is a long general list of titles, which makes the extracting of works of any given composer a very tedious business). The selection of rare photos is generous and fascinating. Joplin's brief *The School of Ragtime; Six Exercises for Piano* (1908) is reproduced and, in the Oak editions, so are 16 complete rags. (A selected list of cylinder recordings appeared in the Knopf and Grove Press [1959] editions but was omitted thereafter.)

45 **CHARTERS, SAMUEL   The Bluesmen. The story and the music of the men who made the Blues**   New York: Oak Publications, 1967   223p   intro   photos   discography ("Records Cited")   index   (reviewed *Ethnomusicology* 12:454-6 Sept 1968)

The author describes this important study of male blues singers as the first in a projected three-volume series on the subject. "This first volume discusses the singers and the styles from Mississippi, Alabama, and Texas up to the second World War, with a brief consideration of the traceable relationships between the blues and African song"— (introduction). The biographical material is derived largely from interviews in the field conducted by "dozens of researchers." There is also frequent musical commentary (with examples) and many complete song texts.

The book is not broad in scope, but it is nicely detailed. The following men receive major attention: Charley Patton, Son House, Skip James, Robert Johnson, Booker T. ("Bukka") White, Blind Lemon Jefferson, Henry Thomas ("Ragtime Texas"), Texas Alexander.

46 **CHARTERS, SAMUEL B.   The Country Blues**   New York: Rinehart, 1959   288p intro   photos   appendix ("Recorded Blues Backgrounds"; "The Blues Recordings") index   (reviewed *Notes* 17:231-2 Mar 1960)

A number of years of original field research were devoted to the preparation of this key work, the first extensive study of early blues singers and their recordings. Charters attempts "to discuss every major blues artist as fully as [he] was able"—(introduction). There are interviews with the singers and their associates and much biographical information throughout.

47 **CHARTERS, SAMUEL BARCLAY, IV   Jazz: New Orleans 1885-1957; An Index to the Negro Musicians of New Orleans**   Belleville, N.J.: Walter C. Allen, 1958   iv, 167p   preface   publisher's foreword   photos   discographies ("Discographical Appendix")   indices (to names of musicians; to names of bands; 3 others)   (Series: *Jazz Monographs No. 2*, February 1958)

_____.   **Jazz: New Orleans 1885-1963 . . .**   Rev. ed.   New York: Oak Publications, 1963   173p   preface   photos   discographies   "An appendix: Some New Source Material on the Beginnings of Jazz in New Orleans"   p155-58   indices (including new index to addenda sections)   (reviewed *Journal of American Folklore* 77:364-5 Oct-Dec 1964)

An excellent biographical dictionary arranged in four chronological sections: 1885-1899; 1899-1919; 1919-1931; 1931- . Each section has an introduction, biographies of individuals, coverage of the brass bands and orchestral groups, and addenda. A one-page note titled "1957" found in the 1st edition was omitted in the 1963 edition (it is no great loss). The 2nd edition "includes new information on a number of musicians, additional biographies, historical material which has only recently come to light, as well as a discussion of some of the newest groups of recordings from New Orleans"– (preface). The photos, appendices, and indices are marvelous.

48 **CHILTON, JOHN   Who's Who in Jazz; Storyville to Swing Street**   London: The Bloomsbury Book Shop, 1970   447p   foreword   intro   photos   bibliography   (newspapers and periodicals from seven countries presumably used in preparing the book)   (reviewed *Storyville* 31:6 Oct-Nov 1970)

"This is an anthology of biographies detailing the careers of over 1,000 musicians whose names are part of jazz history. All the musicians and vocalists given individual entries were born before 1920. Only musicians born or raised in the U.S.A. are in-cluded in this volume"–(introduction). Chilton seems to have been generally con-scientious in seeking out and verifying the details of his subjects' lives and (especially) careers. One does spot, however, occasional lapses and inaccuracies, which I suppose are unavoidable for someone attempting on a large scale to weed fact from fiction among the tangled thickets of jazz history, especially when that someone is himself a jazz musician rather than a scholar or professional researcher.

Nevertheless, the book is valuable for its coverage of numerous little-known figures not accounted for in other sources. Chilton is also particularly good in detailing the fates of his biographees: Did you know that Chick Bullock "is now believed to be running a gas station in California"? that the body of Joe Keyes "was found floating in the Harlem River" in 1950? that Al Killian "was murdered by a psychopathic land-lord"? or that Castor McCord "left professional music in the 1940s and became a hairdresser"? You will find all of these facts and many more in this substantial, if uneven, guide to the older jazzmen.

49   FEATHER, LEONARD   The New Edition of the Encyclopedia of Jazz   Completely revised, enlarged and brought up to date   Appreciations by Duke Ellington, Benny Goodman and John Hammond   New York: Bonanza Books, 1962   527p   (reviewed *Jazz Journal* 14:36 July 1961)

The standard encyclopedia in the jazz field. Biographies of jazz figures cover 378 pages; included are dozens of excellent photos. The balance of the book is devoted to a number of special features, of which the following are outstanding:

- seven extensive essays including "Sixty Years of Jazz: An Historical Survey" and "The Anatomy of Jazz" (good musical examples) by Feather, and "Jazz and Classical Music" (highly recommended) by Gunther Schuller;
- tabulation of international jazz polls;
- annotated discographies (History of Jazz on Records; Recommended Jazz Records);
- lists of jazz organizations, schools, booking agencies, and record companies;
- annotated bibliography (books and periodicals).

An indispensable reference tool.

50   GODRICH, JOHN, and ROBERT M. W. DIXON, compilers   **Blues & Gospel Records 1902-1942**   Rev. ed.   London: Storyville Publications, 1969   912p   intro   indices (of accompanists; of labels and companies mentioned)   (reviewed *Ethnomusicology* 14:3 Sept 1970)

An exhaustive coverage of this field. The compilers state that they have "attempted to list every distinctively Negroid folk music record made up to the end of 1942"– (introduction). The book is arranged alphabetically by solo performer or group; complete discographical information is provided for each title. The opening commentaries, which "give a rough general overview of the activities of some of the record companies involved in the field of blues and gospel recording," are of much interest. The 18-page section on long-playing records is very helpful.

51   HORRICKS, RAYMOND   **These Jazzmen of Our Time**   London: Victor Gollancz, 1959   236p   intro ("A Pocketful of Blues")   photos   index   (reviewed *Jazz Monthly* 5:29 Dec 1959)

Fair biographical coverage and generally astute critical evaluation of the work of 16 modern jazz figures: Thelonious Monk, Miles Davis, J. J. Johnson, Gerry Mulligan, Bud Powell, Gil Evans, Milt Jackson, John Lewis, Max Roach, Art Blakey, Jimmy Giuffre, Dave Brubeck, Charles Mingus, Gigi Gryce, Sonny Rollins, and Quincy Jones. Eight of the essays are by Horricks, the balance by Alan Morgan, Nat Hentoff, Martin Williams, and four others. The portrait photos, by Herman Leonard, are excellent.

52   JEPSEN, JORGEN GRUNNET   **Jazz Records 1942-1962; A Discography**   Holte, Denmark: Karl Emil Knudsen, 1963-1971   8 vols.   (reviewed *Jazz Hot* 196:17 Mar 1964; *Jazz Monthly* 9:5 Feb 1964, 10:25-6 Nov 1964)

The definitive jazz discography for the years covered. Each volume has a foreword, explanatory notes, and discographical information arranged alphabetically by artist. The information given is extensive: personnel, matrix numbers, recording dates, recording place, release numbers. Both European and American releases are included. Three categories of recordings are excluded: gospel and religious; vocal ensembles (especially in the rhythm-and-blues field); semi-jazz recordings.

Note: The final volume of this set to be published, vol. 4, is in four separate issues marked 4a, 4b, 4c and 4d. The dates in the title of this volume read 1942-1967.

53 KEEPNEWS, ORRIN, and BILL GRAUER, JR. A Pictorial History of Jazz; People and Places from New Orleans to Modern Jazz London: Spring Books, 1955 282p

————————————————. Text and Captions by Orrin Keepnews New ed. rev. by Orrin Keepnews New York: Crown, 1966 297p intro index (reviewed *Down Beat* 33:38 Oct 20 1966)

". . . we make no claim to a 'complete' history. There are inevitable gaps. . . . Allow us to note, then, that the first word of our title is not 'The,' but 'A' "—(introduction).

There are other good picture-books in jazz, such as *New Orleans Jazz; A Family Album* by Al Rose and Edmond Souchon (Baton Rouge: Louisiana State University Press, 1967), but this one offers the broadest scope. Both the commentary and choice of visual material are informed by meticulous research. The American edition is superior not only because it contains more pictures but because the quality of paper and reproduction is greatly improved over the original.

54 REISNER, ROBERT GEORGE, compiler The Literature of Jazz; a preliminary bibliography With an introduction by Marshall W. Stearns New York: The New York Public Library, 1954 [Reprinted from the *Bulletin of The New York Public Library* March-May 1954] 53p compiler's note

————————————————. **The Literature of Jazz; a selective bibliography** Second ed., rev. and enl. 1959 63p (reviewed *Notes* 16:567 Sept 1959)

In three sections: books about various aspects of jazz (biographies, fiction, etc.); background books; selective list of magazine references (a few newspaper references are also included). Reisner also provides a list of magazines devoted wholly or principally to jazz.

This is a fine, detailed compilation. Some students may find it limited, however, because of the difficulty in locating articles and books on a given subject. Except for references to articles in **Current Biography (3)**, all entries are alphabetical by author. This means that if you look up, say, Eddie Condon, you will find several references to articles written by him; however, if you wanted an article *about* him you would have to know to look under the name Robert Sylvester, the author of "The barefoot boy and his band," a Condon profile.

55   **RUST, BRIAN, compiler**   **Jazz Records A-Z, 1897-1931**   Hatch End, Middlesex, England: Published by the author, c1961   736p   intro   (reviewed *Metronome* 78:18-19 Aug 1961)

                          _____.   **Jazz Records A-Z, 1932-1942**   No place; no publisher; no date   680p   intro   (reviewed *Jazz Monthly* 12:5-6 Mar 1966)

These two valuable discographies form a set and are generally referred to as vol. 1 and vol. 2. With **Jepsen (52)** as companion, they contribute to comprehensive coverage of jazz recordings made between 1897 and 1967 (the **Sonneck-Upton** and **Wolfe** of the jazz world!).

The information is exhaustive: record and matrix numbers, date of recording, personnel, etc. Exemplary.

56   **SHAPIRO, NAT, and NAT HENTOFF, eds.**   **Hear Me Talkin' to Ya; The Story of Jazz by the Men Who Made It**   New York: Rinehart, 1955   xvi, 432p   intro "Selected Long-Playing Records" p411-13   index   (*R* Dover Publications) (reviewed *Notes* 13:59-61 Dec 1955)

One hundred fifty-three contributors are represented in this informal collection of anecdotes and reminiscences. Much of the material is from interviews conducted by Shapiro and Hentoff: "The conversations took place in night clubs and bars, in offices, on the sidewalk between sets, and in homes. There were also letters, tape recordings, and telephone conversations"—(introduction). The compilers also drew on interviews and autobiographical pieces previously published in magazines, newspapers, and books.

Excerpts from the various source materials are grouped by subject within a chronological framework (New Orleans at the turn of the century to the West Coast scene in the mid-1950s). Though cities, changing styles, and other topics (e.g., drug addiction in the jazz world) are discussed, the book deals largely with the careers and contributions of individual musicians. The interviewees' comments about themselves and their colleagues are informative, often amusing, and occasionally revelatory. The sections on Bessie Smith and Bix Beiderbecke are particularly interesting.

57 SHAPIRO, NAT, and NAT HENTOFF, eds.   The Jazz Makers   New York: Rinehart, 1957   xiii, 368p   "About the Authors" p xi   photos   discographies (at ends of chapters)   index   (reviewed *Notes* 15:402-3 June 1958)

This is an anthology of 21 original essays by 10 jazz authorities, some of whom "chose to bear strongly on biography; others were more concerned with analysis of the musical achievements of the man. Several combined both approaches. The main goal for all . . . was to communicate something of the personality of each of these jazz makers"— (preface).

The 21 performers are representative of the major movements and styles in jazz, ranging from "New Orleans" to "Progressive." Here are the names: Jelly Roll Morton, Warren "Baby" Dodds, Louis Armstrong, Jack Teagarden, Earl Hines, Bix Beiderbecke, Pee Wee Russell, Bessie Smith, Thomas "Fats" Waller, Art Tatum, Coleman Hawkins, Benny Goodman, Duke Ellington, Charlie Parker, Fletcher Henderson, William "Count" Basie, Lester Young, Billie Holiday, Roy Eldridge, Charlie Christian, and John "Dizzy" Gillespie.

58   WILLIAMS, MARTIN, general ed.   The Macmillan Jazz Masters Series   New York:
The Macmillan Co.;   London: Collier-Macmillan Ltd.

The monographs in this series are by reputable and knowledgeable commentators in
their field. As in so much of the jazz literature, however, certain scholarly niceties
have generally been omitted. Do not look for detailed citations for quoted or corrobo-
rating materials: the authors have not cluttered their texts with footnotes. Personal
interviews, so important in historical jazz research, are the source of many quotations
throughout the series. The accuracy of these quotes must be taken largely on faith:
one must depend here upon the veracity of the authors. Fortunately, Williams has
chosen his men carefully, and the overall quality of the series is generally high.

58a   GITLER, IRA   Jazz Masters of the Forties (1966)   290p   intro   discographies ("Recommended Listening") at end of each section   bibliography
photos   index   (reviewed *Music Journal* 24:105 Sept 1966)

The author states: "The music and players that came to light in the forties,
typifying the period, are the subject of this book. The discussion not only
encompasses what the major figures accomplished in the forties, but follows
their careers into the sixties—or, in some cases, to their premature ends"—
(introduction). All of the major figures of the period are given extensive biographical and critical treatment in individual chapters; many other contemporary musicians (including arrangers) are also featured. Full of careful research,
sensitive treatment, and intelligent opinion. The most substantial and dependable single account of the period in published form. Included: Charlie Parker,
Dizzy Gillespie, Bud Powell, J. J. Johnson, Oscar Pettiford, Kenny Clarke, Max
Roach, Dexter Gordon, Lennie Tristano, Lee Konitz, and Tadd Dameron.

58b   GOLDBERG, JOE   Jazz Masters of the Fifties (1965)   246p   intro   selected discography at end of each section   (reviewed *Down Beat* 32:39 July
15 1965)

Twelve excellent original biographical-critical essays of 14 to 26 pages each.
Goldberg makes up his pieces from a judicious mixture of secondary sources,

personal interviews, and first-hand experience. Many biographical details can be found nowhere else. Included: Gerry Mulligan, Thelonious Monk, Art Blakey, Miles Davis, Sonny Rollins, The Modern Jazz Quartet, Charles Mingus, Paul Desmond, Ray Charles, John Coltrane, Cecil Taylor, and Ornette Coleman.

58c HADLOCK, RICHARD   Jazz Masters of the Twenties (1965)   255p   intro discographies ("Recommended Listening") and bibliographies ("Recommended Reading") at end of each section   photos   (reviewed *Jazz Journal* 18:24-5 Oct 1965)

Because so many of the musicians of this period have been covered extensively in other sources, the author seems to assume that any reader using his book is forearmed with considerable background knowledge. Specific biographical information is scant (the first concrete fact we are given about the life of Louis Armstrong is that he was "fresh out of the waifs' home at 14"). The apparent (but unstated) purpose here is to give career information (*X* played in *Y*'s band before playing in *Z*'s band) and criticism. With limitations, then, the book focuses on Louis Armstrong from 1924 to 1931, Earl Hines, Bix Beiderbecke, Fats Waller, James P. Johnson, Jack Teagarden, Fletcher Henderson, Don Redman, Bessie Smith, and Eddie Lang. A chapter entitled "The Chicagoans" lumps together Benny Goodman, Dave Tough, and many others; since the sequence here is jumbled it is difficult to follow the path of any one figure.

58d STEWART, REX   Jazz Masters of the Thirties (1972)   223p   foreword (by Martin Williams)   photos   appendices

This volume of the Macmillan series is a posthumous collection of Stewart's relaxed anecdotal pieces which originally appeared in *Down Beat, Evergreen Review, Music Maker,* and *Melody Maker.* The author was a highly regarded trumpeter in the Fletcher Henderson and Duke Ellington orchestras, among others. He was also a charming writer, giving shrewd eye-witness accounts and low-keyed criticism, and occasionally sketching in background information. The pieces do not really provide a rounded coverage of jazz figures in the 1930s, yet they form perhaps the most distinctive work in the series. I only wish the book had been indexed.

The appendices contain a good essay on Count Basie by Hsio Wen Shih and an appreciation of the author by composer Francis Thorne. Included: Jean Goldkette, Fletcher Henderson, Louis Armstrong, Jimmy Harrison, Coleman Hawkins, Red Norvo, Duke Ellington, Joe Nanton, Barney Bigard, Ben Webster, Harry Carney, John Kirby, Sidney Catlett, Benny Carter, Art Tatum, and Count Basie.

58e   WILLIAMS, MARTIN   Jazz Masters in Transition, 1957-69 (1970)   288p preface   photos

A collection of 87 of Williams's "reviews, interviews, brief profiles, and narratives of such events as rehearsals, recording dates, television tapings, and evenings in night clubs." All are fairly short and appeared previously in *The New York Times, Down Beat, Saturday Review*, and other sources.

58f   WILLIAMS, MARTIN   Jazz Masters of New Orleans (1967)   xvii, 287p intro   annotated discographies ("Recordings") and bibliographies ("References") at end of each section   photos   index   (reviewed *Music Journal* 25:60 May 1967)

Colorful, well-investigated essays on two bands and nine individuals either born in New Orleans or closely associated with early New Orleans jazz. Williams's stated intention is to go back to the music, "to rehear it in the light of both subsequent research into its history and of subsequent developments in jazz, [and] to fill in some gaps in previous histories." Biographical information is sound if sketchy. Coverage: Buddy Bolden, Original Dixieland Jazz Band, Ferdinand ("Jelly Roll") Morton, Joseph ("King") Oliver, New Orleans Rhythm Kings, Sidney Bechet, Louis Armstrong, Arthur ("Zutty") Singleton, Edward ("Kid") Ory, Willie Gary ("Bunk") Johnson, and Henry James ("Red") Allen, Jr.

Pop Music (including Stage and Film Music)

59   **The ASCAP Biographical Dictionary of Composers, Authors and Publishers** 1966
Edition   Compiled and edited by The Lynn Farnol Group, Inc. New York: The
American Society of Composers, Authors and Publishers, 1966 845p foreword
(by Stanley Adams) preface "ASCAP Publisher Members" p815-45 (reviewed
Variety 245:48 Dec 28 1966)

Brief biographies of over 5000 ASCAP members, alive and deceased. A list of representative song and show credits is given with each entry. The book is the largest single source of biographical information in the pop-music field (many classical-com-
poser members of ASCAP are also included). It should be remembered, however,
that the coverage, while generous, is selective: the entire ASCAP membership numbers far more than 5000. Also, some of the biographies contain errors.

60 **BURTON, JACK**   **[The Blue Book Series]** Watkins Glen, N.Y.: Century House

The three basic books in this well-known series are in general badly organized, inade-
quately indexed, and otherwise stained by sins of omission and commission. No publishers are listed. All "facts" should be verified in other sources, e.g. **Shapiro (71)**,
Lewine (66), Green (65). Nevertheless, the range of the Blue Books is wide, and they
are useful.

60a   _____. **The Blue Book of Broadway Musicals**
With additions by Larry Freeman (1952, 1969) 327p foreword photos
indices (of show titles)

The Broadway book is arranged by decade, and within a decade by composer,
which means that listings for many composers are scattered over several sections (a nuisance). Authors of book and lyrics are identified, as are the original

leading players; representative songs are listed. A general introduction precedes
the listings for each decade.

The book first appeared in 1952. The edition described here retains the earlier
sections virtually intact: "It is realized that errors in Mr. Burton's original compilation will remain in this re-issue; but . . . an effort has been made to correct
by insert"–(p4). A brief new section covering 1951-69 is tacked on at the end.

60b   _____. **The Blue Book of Hollywood Musicals**
Songs from the Sound Tracks and the Stars Who Sang Them Since the Birth of
the Talkies a Quarter-Century Ago (1953)   296p   foreword   photos
"Songs Awarded The Oscar and 'Golden Circle' Musicals" p4   "Record Albums
of Hollywood Musicals" p280   index (of movie titles)

Listing of films by year of release; composer, lyricist, leading players, representative songs; brief introduction to each year. Includes musicals, feature films
with songs, feature cartoons with songs.

60c   _____. **The Blue Book of Tin Pan Alley**   A Human
Interest Anthology of American Popular Music   (first printing 1950, c1951)
520p   foreword   photos   indices (of composers; of lyricists)   (reviewed
Notes 19:130-1 Dec 1951)

Arranged by decade (with introductions), then by composer (with brief biographical sketches). The information on recordings is helpful.

But what is a "human interest anthology"?

60d   _____. **The Index of American Popular Music**
Thousands of titles cross-referenced to our basic anthologies of popular songs
(1957)   unpaged

This is an index to the song titles in the three **Blue Books** as well as in a minor
collection, *The Melodies Linger On*, by Larry Freeman (Watkins Glen, N.Y.:
Century House, 1951). Since none of the books includes its own song index,
this volume is essential to the set.

61 ENGEL, LEHMAN The American Musical Theater; A Consideration [New York]: A CBS Legacy Collection Book, distributed by the Macmillan Co., 1967 xiii, 236p intro (by Brooks Atkinson) preface photos appendices bibliography index (reviewed *Notes* 25:244-5 Dec 1968)

This is primarily a collection of rare photos of stars, composers, and productions, but it contains also an excellent historical and analytical "consideration" by Engel, an experienced Broadway conductor and teacher. It was originally issued with a Columbia recording of the same title. The three appendices are a bonus: 1) discography (I wish more detail had been included); 2) published librettos (a good but partial listing; lacks publishing details); 3) published vocal scores (probably the best list around, but no publication data; cf. **Lewine [66]**). The bibliography is small.

62 EWEN, DAVID New Complete Book of the American Musical Theater New York: Holt, Rinehart and Winston, 1970 xxv, 800p preface intro photos appendices index (reviewed *Jazz and Pop* 10:41 Mar 1971)

I quote from my review of this book in *Library Journal* (May 1 1971):

> Enlarged from the *Complete Book of the American Musical Theater* (1958; rev. ed. 1959), this edition may be new but it is certainly not complete. Ewen and his publishers continually invite gunfire by setting up such obvious clay pigeons as this. No foreign shows are included. The credits and casts for each show are not complete. There are no complete lists of songs for the shows. Almost in spite of itself, however, the book does have much to offer: generally accurate basic data on a liberal sampling of musicals from 1866 (*The Black Crook*) to 1970 (*Applause*); biographical sketches of many lyricists, composers, and librettists (a number of whom are relatively obscure and hard to locate); chronology of shows covered in the book; a handy list of best-known songs with pertinent data; and a good index to the whole. . . .

63 FREDERICKS, VIC Who's Who in Rock 'n Roll; Facts, Fotos and Fan Gossip About the Performers in the World of Rock 'n Roll New York: Frederick Fell, 1958 96p

This is actually a fan magazine gotten up (no doubt) largely from press-agent material. The articles on Presley and the emergence of rock are not bad, however. Noted here because of its relatively early publication date. Those "fotos" are awful.

64 FULD, JAMES   American Popular Music (Reference Book) 1875-1950   Philadelphia: Musical Americana, 1955   94p   intro   plates   index (general)   (reviewed *Notes* 12: 595-6 Sept 1955)

_____.   Supplement to American Popular Music . . . (1956)   9p

Carefully prepared descriptive bibliography of first editions. Highly selective. A warm-up for **The Book of World-Famous Music (7).** The list of pseudonyms of leading pop composers is useful. The **Supplement** is not indexed.

65 GREEN, STANLEY   The World of Musical Comedy   The story of the American musical stage as told through the careers of its foremost composers and lyricists. Foreword by Deems Taylor   New York: Ziff-Davis, 1960   xvi, 391p   preface appendix   index   (reviewed *Musical America* 81:43 Oct 1961)

In two sections: the first provides good articles with biographical/career information on composers and lyricists, arranged in chronological order from Victor Herbert to Rick Besoyan; the second, contained in the appendix, gives a list of works of each composer covered (same chronological arrangement as first section). Extensive information for each show: author of book and lyrics; opening date; number of performances; cast; principal songs; briefly annotated discographies.

Three flaws: the chronological arrangement is an annoyance, especially in the appendix; the index is inadequate (references to songs are given only for the first section; the important appendix is not indexed); and there is no publication information for the songs.

The composers and lyricists, in alphabetical order, are:

Adler, Richard	Lane, Burton
Arlen, Harold	Lerner, Alan Jay
Berlin, Irving	Loesser, Frank
Bernstein, Leonard	Loewe, Frederick
Cohan, George M.	Porter, Cole
Dietz, Howard	Rodgers, Richard
Duke, Vernon	Romberg, Sigmund
Friml, Rudolf	Rome, Harold
Gershwin, George	Ross, Jerry
Hammerstein, Oscar II	Schwartz, Arthur
Harburg, E. Y.	Styne, Jule
Hart, Lorenz	Weill, Kurt
Herbert, Victor	Willson, Meredith
Kern, Jerome	Youmans, Vincent

66 **LEWINE, RICHARD, and ALFRED SIMON** **Encyclopedia of Theatre Music** A comprehensive listing of more than 4000 songs from Broadway and Hollywood: 1900-1960 New York: Random House, 1961 vii, 247p preface index (reviewed *Music Journal* 20:59 May 1962)

An alphabetical title index of songs. The movie songs are in a separate section. Composer, lyricist, show or movie source, and date are given with each title. There is a "Show Chronology 1925-1960" which does not give as much information as **Green (65).** One excellent feature is a listing of published vocal scores for musicals (prior to 1961) with dates of publication (but without publishers).

67 **McCARTY, CLIFFORD, compiler and ed.** **Film Composers in America; A Checklist of Their Work** Foreword by Lawrence Morton Glendale, Calif.: distributed by John Valentine, 1953 xx, 193p preface "Academy Awards" p143-44 index (of film titles) (reviewed *Notes* 11:105 Dec 1953)

This is a straightforward alphabetical list of composers, with titles of their American film scores; the year of release and the studio are indicated for each title. Though McCarty's compilation offers only a minimum of information, it may easily satisfy the needs of the music student if not the movie buff.

The book was published in a limited edition of 400 copies and is hard to come by. I wish a new updated edition would be published in a big run. It is a useful work.

68   **ROHDE, H. KANDY, ed.   The Gold Of Rock & Roll 1955-1967**   With research assistance by Laing Ned Kandel   New York: Arbor House, 1970   352p   intro photos   bibliography (sources used)   song title index   artist index   (reviewed *Journal of Popular Culture* 4:981-84 no. 2, Spring 1971)

A chronology of hit records. Separate section for each year, including: general introduction to the events and pop-music trends of the year (the writing here can be pretty funny, as in "Paul Anka was short and not sexy looking like Fabian, but he wrote his own songs and they were consistently good."); photo of a leading singer or group; a list of the top 50 records of the year (with performers); a listing of the top 10 records for each week of the year. Information in the latter section includes performer, writers, record label and number, publisher of the sheet music, and the licensing organization.

My friend Ian Whitcomb, British rock singer turned author, tells me that while Rohde's weekly listings are dependable, the top-50 lists are occasionally capricious. One would do well to use other sources (the *Billboard* magazine charts, for instance) for these statistics.

69   **ROXON, LILLIAN   Lillian Roxon's Rock Encyclopedia**   A Workman Publishing Co. Book   New York: Grosset & Dunlap, 1969   611p   photos   appendix (Cash Box top albums 1960-1968; Cash Box top singles 1949-1968)   (reviewed *Saturday Review* 52:50 Dec 6 1969)

"I wanted to record the facts without losing the feelings"–(Author's Note).

The feelings are much in evidence, but where are all the facts? For each performer or group mentioned we are given lists of albums (with contents) and singles, frequently with date of release; however, label identification and record numbers are omitted.

Why? Specific biographical information is all but non-existent. Typical is the conclusion of the brief Buffy Sainte-Marie article: "Buffy, who grew up in Maine, moved into the folk places of New York in 1963. She is now one of the giants of the contemporary folk circuit." (Compare with the article on Sainte-Marie in **Stambler [38]**.)

This collection (scratch the word encyclopedia) may provide some entertaining moments for bedtime reading, otherwise forget it.

70 SALEM, JAMES M.   A Guide to Critical Reviews. Part II: The Musical From Rodgers-And-Hart to Lerner-And-Loewe   Metuchen, N.J.: The Scarecrow Press, 1967   353p   foreword   indices   (reviewed *Notes* 25:245-46 Dec 1968)

"This bibliography is the second part of a projected four-volume series under the general title *A Guide to Critical Reviews*"–(foreword). This is the only part to deal with musical shows. Reviews are cited for shows on Broadway between the 1920-21 and 1964-65 seasons. Sources are American and Canadian periodicals and *The New York Times*.

The shows are arranged alphabetically within each season. The credits are extensive for each show: composer, author, lyricist, director, designer, choreographer, number of performances, and opening date. The supplemental lists of long-running musicals, New York Drama Critics' Circle award winners, and Pulitzer Prize winners are handy. The four indices are generous and useful: authors, composers, lyricists; directors, designers, choreographers; titles of works adapted as musicals, with names of the original authors; and titles of musicals.

The book has one unfortunate flaw: the coverage between 1920-21 and 1927-28 is highly selective (works by only 11 of the most famous composers and lyricists are represented). This means that the work of several interesting black figures of this period are eliminated: James P. Johnson, Clarence and Spencer Williams, Eubie Blake, Cecil Mack, and others. Also eliminated are works by Henderson-De Sylva-Brown, Billy Rose, and Bert Kalmar-Harry Ruby.

71 SHAPIRO, NAT, ed.   Popular Music; An Annotated Index of American Popular Songs   New York: Adrian Press

— vol. 1 *1950-1959*   (1964)   xiii, 345p   intro ("About the Book and
How To Use It")
— vol. 2 *1940-1949*   (1965)   xiii, 347p   intro ("About the Book . . .")
"Popular Music in the 1940's" p3
— vol. 3 *1960-1964*   (1967)   xiii, 335p   intro ("About the Book . . .")
"Popular Music, 1960-1964" p1
— vol. 4 *1930-1939*   (1968)   xiii, 335p   intro ("About the Book . . .")
"Popular Music in the 1930's" p1
— vol. 5 *1920-1929*   With introductions by Nat Shapiro, Miles Kreuger,
and Frank Driggs   (1969)   331p   intro ("About the Book . . .")
"Popular Music in the 1920's" by Shapiro; "Theater and Film Music"
by Kreuger; "Jazz" by Driggs   (reviewed *Jazz Journal* 17:11 Oct
1964; *Billboard* 77:16 Nov 20 1965)

Shapiro does not boast idly when he states in his introduction to vol. 1 that this
series, when complete, will be a "comprehensive, selective documentation of American popular songs of the twentieth century." Judging from the five volumes published so far, it will be just that. It is already the best tool of its kind in existence.

In dealing with such a compilation, one inevitably must raise the question: what
were the criteria involved in selecting the songs to be included? Here is Shapiro's
answer: ". . . it was the purpose of *Popular Music* to document those musical works
which 1) achieved a substantial degree of popular acceptance, 2) were exposed to
the public in especially notable circumstances, or 3) were accepted and given important performances by influential musical and dramatic artists."

Most entries come with voluminous information: authors; composers; publishers;
historical notes; anecdotes; data on foreign, folk, and classical origins; identification
of theatrical, film, and radio introducers of songs, and of any other performers identified with the songs. First or best-selling recordings are also indicated.

Here is a sample entry from 1926:
CHARMAINE
Words and music by Erno Rapee and Lew Pollack
Miller Music Corporation
Melody composed by Rapee in Hungary in 1913. Theme song of
What Price Glory (film). Performed by Harry James and his
Orchestra in *Two Girls and a Sailor* (film, 1944). Best-selling
record in 1951 by Mantovani (London).

Each volume concludes with a list of *current* publishers (with addresses) represented in the volume, and a song-title index. My only quibble in the face of Shapiro's excellence is that there is no name index; this means, for instance, that one cannot locate all Cole Porter songs listed in, say, the 1930s volume by consulting his name in an index.

72 **SMOLIAN, STEVEN, compiler   A Handbook of Film, Theater, and Television Music on Record, 1948-1969**   New York: The Record Undertaker, 1970   64p "The Collector's Record Market" p9   intro   index (separate vol., 64p)   (reviewed *Notes* 28:3 Mar 1972)

The first of the two slight volumes which comprise this handbook is a discography: soundtrack and/or original-cast long-playing recordings listed by show title with pertinent data (the performer credits are selective). The second volume contains indices of the record manufacturers and composers. The set serves as a superb adjunct to work in the field of American stage, TV, and movie music.

The inclusion of the manufacturers index and a "Record Market" section suggests that the handbook was intended primarily for collectors; a performer index would better serve the student and layman. Highly useful, nevertheless.

73 **SPAETH, SIGMUND   A History of Popular Music in America**   New York: Random House, 1948   xv, 729p   preface   intro   "Additional Popular Music from Colonial Times to the Present" p587-657   bibliography   index   (reviewed *Metronome* 65:23 Feb 1949)

This is more a chronology than a history, but it is a good one. Each chapter, usually covering a decade, is packed with data on who wrote what when, who sang the songs, which were hits and which weren't, anecdotes and biographical bits. No real analysis is attempted, as it is in **Wilder (75)**.

Good index as far as it goes, but that is not far enough: the useful 70-page compilation of additional music, arranged by year of copyright, is not indexed.

74 **WALKER, LEO   The Wonderful Era of the Great Dance Bands**   Berkeley, Calif.: Howell-North Books, 1964   315p   preface   photos   illus   index   (reviewed *International Musician* 63:26 Dec 1964)

Primarily a picture book, and a good one. The commentary provides information on the history of the big-band era (roughly 1930-50), personnel of bands, and careers of individual musicians.

75 **WILDER, ALEC**   **American Popular Song; The Great Innovators, 1900-1950**   Edited and with an Introduction by James T. Maher   New York: Oxford University Press, 1972   xxxix, 536p   indices of songs cited, lyricists, composers

While this book does not contain much straight biographical information, it discusses in detail the songs of 11 composers in chronological sequence within each man's career. The work of 12 others is discussed in one 82-page chapter. Another chapter is devoted to individual songs published between 1920 and 1950 that Wilder considers outstanding. The book should be a necessary component of any study of these chosen "innovators." Wilder's analyses are sophisticated, unequivocal, witty. They are the product of long study and wide experience coupled with intelligence and sensitivity. Musical examples appear in lavish profusion.

The 11 major composers: Kern; Berlin; Gershwin; Rodgers; Porter; Arlen; Youmans and Schwartz; Burton Lane, Hugh Martin, and Vernon Duke.

Church Music

76 **DANIEL, RALPH T.**   **The Anthem in New England before 1800**   Evanston, Ill.: Northwestern University Press, 1966   xvi, 282p   foreword (by George Howerton) preface   illus   appendices   bibliography   musical supplement   index   (Series: *Pi Kappa Lambda Studies in American Music*)   (reviewed *Inter-American Institute for Musical Research Yearbook* 2:186 1966)

A splendid study, included here for its biographical information on anthem composers (with lists of works), appendices, excellent bibliography (books, articles, manu-scripts, and music), and musical supplement of 14 anthems.

77 **ELLINWOOD, LEONARD**   **The History of American Church Music**   New York: Morehouse-Gorham, 1953   xiv, 274p   preface   plates   photos   appendices ("The Organists of Trinity Parish, New York City" "Selected Music Lists" "Biog-raphies of American Church Musicians" "Notes and Bibliography")   index   (*R* Da Capo Press)   (reviewed *Notes* 11:308 Mar 1954)

No author should open the door to unnecessary criticism by calling his book "the" history of anything. Ellinwood produced here a conscientious and solemn coverage, but it is not *the* history of American church music—a history which does not exist at the moment.

The pertinent features of the book are the biographical appendix (which covers 40 pages) on church composers, tune book compilers, etc., and the interesting bibliog-raphical appendix.

78 **METCALF, FRANK J.**   **American Writers and Compilers of Sacred Music**   New York: The Abingdon Press, 1925   373p   preface   illus   index   (*R* Russel & Russell)

Though a great deal of work has been done in this area since 1925, **Metcalf** stands as a classic and is still useful. Contains over 100 biographical sketches arranged chronologically from John Tufts (*b* 1689) to Samuel Ward (*d* 1903). Bibliographi-cal information.

79 **STEVENSON, ROBERT**   **Protestant Church Music in America; A Short Survey of Men and Movements from 1564 to the Present**   New York: W. W. Norton & Company, 1966   xiii, 168p   preface   plates   bibliography   index   (reviewed *Notes* 23:520 Mar 1967)

This compact "résumé" (to use the author's term) is the best work in its field as of 1972. Stevenson states that because his aim was "to provide a compressed text for use in seminaries, choir schools, and colleges, I have had to omit much important data and have been obliged to consign many men and movements to a mere passing mention"—(p xi). This lack is more than offset by the tremendously rich and detailed bibliographical and biographical footnotes. Here the student is repeatedly led to the primary sources; only the original documents, Stevenson states, can clear up "a stream still muddied with the mere opinions of such nineteenth-century partisans as Hood, Gould, and Ritter"—(p xii).

(While agreeing wholeheartedly with this idea, I must say as an aside that Stevenson could have somewhat vivified his "compressed text" with a few "mere opinions" of his own rather than constantly quoting those of others, an action which seems purely an academic reflex.)

The large bibliography includes materials in the "ML" classification (books about music) in the Library of Congress system, theses and dissertations, and "books outside the field of music that have nonetheless offered useful documentation." The quality of this section matches that of the text: distinguished and highly informative.

Opera

80 HIPSHER, EDWARD ELLSWORTH   American Opera and Its Composers   A Complete History of Serious American Opera, with a Summary of the lighter forms which led up to its birth.   Philadelphia: Theodore Presser Co., 1927   xi, 408p intro ("Prologue")   bibliography (of works consulted)   index

——————————————————————. (1934)   ix, 478p

I have it on good authority that this book, long regarded the standard work on the subject, is seriously marred by extensive factual errors. Barton Cantrell, who has conducted exhaustive research in earlier American opera for several years, began with **Hipsher** as a guide but soon found that it could not be trusted. For accurate, authoritative treatment of this most intriguing subject, we will have to wait for Cantrell's own book.

81 **SONNECK, O. G. Early Opera in America** New York: G. Schirmer, 1915 viii, 230p prefatory note plates illus index (*R* Benjamin Bloom)

This is the second book to result from Sonneck's painstaking search of American newspapers and documents for evidence of early musical activities. (See **Sonneck (23)** for comments on the companion book.) It contains data he found on opera production in several key centers before 1800. Two notable features are the extensive charts of operas, with dates of performances, and the bibliographical references found throughout the text.

The apathy of book publishers regarding Sonneck's work seriously affected the shape, style, and scope of this important book. Most of the material first appeared in serial form in *The Music Review* in 1907 and 1908. "The book had grown too bulky for magazine purposes," Sonneck states, "notwithstanding a merciless pruning of my material and a persistent effort at condensation. . . . Had this survey of Early Opera in America originally not been intended for serial publication . . . it would easily have assumed the proportions of my pendant book on 'Early Concert-Life in America' "—(p v). By the time a publisher finally decided to bring out the material in book form, "pressing duties absolutely forbade the revision of the manuscript."

Women in Music

82 **BARNES, EDWIN N. C. American Women in Creative Music** Washington, D.C.: Music Education Publications, 1936 44p bibliography ("Biographical Cross-reference" p43) index (Series: *Tuning in on American Music*)

As opposed to women in the uncreative kind? Trashy pamphlet useful only as a source of names for further research. The biographical sketches (such as they are) are arranged in no discernible order.

83 **SMITH, JULIA, compiler and ed.**   **Directory of American Women Composers**
With selected music for Senior & Junior Clubs   First ed.   [Chicago]: The National
Federation of Music Clubs, 1970   iv, 51p   foreword   (reviewed *Pan Pipes* 63:38
no. 2 1971)

Ms. Smith states the ultimate goal of her work in strong terms: "This *Directory,*
perhaps a 'first of its kind' in the entire world, was conceived to add to the recognition and performance of music by women composers who, along with other women
of the world, aspire to more than their traditional occupations as propagators of the
species and drudges for mankind"—(foreword).

Apart from this (only time can tell whether it will add to recognition and performance), the *Directory* succeeds at another fine, if less ambitious, purpose: it assembles
in one compact volume the names, addresses, and types of music composed (with
publishers' names) of over 600 women composers, both living and deceased. Discreet-
ly, dates are given only for those in the latter category. State of birth and professional
affiliation are indicated for most of the composers. The compilation was derived largely from lists provided by the 50 state presidents of The National Federation of Music
Clubs. It encompasses a wide variety of composers, among whom are a number of
known propagators of the species but apparently no confessed drudges. They range
from Mildred J. Hill (composer of *Happy Birthday to You*), Effie Canning (*Rock-a-bye-
Baby*), Queen Liliuokalani (*Aloha Oe*; for some reason her first name, Lydia, and dates,
1838-1917, are omitted), to Pauline Oliveros (electronic), Beatrice Witkin (12-tone),
and such popular singer-composers as Ella Fitzgerald, Nina Simone, and Julie London
(Peggy Lee, however, being overlooked).

At the risk of being branded a male chauvinist, I will offer a few asides:
 — If an entry such as "SAWYER, ELIZABETH (Betty)" seems
    clear enough, it follows logically that "MAMLOK, URSULA
    (Lewis)" refers to a woman whose nickname is Lewis, which
    is charming if true.
 — Unlike Peggy Glanville-Hicks (properly listed under "G"),
    Ruth Crawford Seeger does not have a hyphenated name and
    should be under "S" instead of "C." Her dates are 1901-1953.
 — Florence Wickham's dates are 1882-1962; her manuscripts are
    at Music Division, The New York Public Library. Ethel
    Leginska's dates are 1886-1970.
 — The manuscript of Mrs. H. H. A. Beach's unpublished opera

Cabildo, once believed lost, is at the Institute for Studies in American Music, University of Missouri-Kansas City.

20th-Century Music

84 CONTEMPORARY MUSIC PROJECT FOR CREATIVITY IN MUSIC EDUCATION (CMP)/MUSIC EDUCATORS NATIONAL CONFERENCE The CMP Library
2nd ed. Vera Brodsky Lawrence, ed. Washington, D.C.: CMP, 1969

> Vol. 1 Works for Band, Winds and Percussion. Solos
> Vol. 2 Works for Orchestra and String Instruments
> Vol. 3 Works for Chorus and Voice

The background of this interesting set is explained in the introduction by Norman Dello Joio and Robert J. Werner:

> During the period 1959 through 1969 the Contemporary Music
> Project, under three grants from the Ford Foundation to the
> Music Educators National Conference, placed seventy-three com-
> posers in residence in seventy-seven selected public school systems
> throughout the United States. One of the tangible results of this
> program is the CMP LIBRARY, which represents a large part of
> the music written especially for the school performing groups to
> which the composers were assigned.

The title of the set may be confusing: the CMP Library of scores exists on micro-film at CMP headquarters in Washington; the three volumes form a catalog of "compositions selected by the composers themselves as representative of their work during their participation in the Composers in Public Schools Program. In some cases composers have also selected works that were not written for the Program, but that they considered suitable for inclusion . . ."–(How To Use The Catalog). The set also contains lists of all works written for the Program during its ten-year duration.

The source-material here is abundant; it includes biographical information on each composer, lists of works, descriptive notes on each composition, representative score pages in miniature, and a complete index in each volume.

The physical form of the set is a bit cumbersome: three large loose-leaf binders with unnumbered leaves.

Composers included:

Albert, Stephen
Angelini, Louis

Bates, David S.
Becker, Frank
Beglarian, Grant
Bielawa, Herbert
Borden, David R.
Brazinski, Frank W.
Briccetti, Thomas B.
Burkley, Bruce H.

Cervone, D. Donald
Chance, John Barnes
Chorbajian, John
Coker, Wilson

Davison, John
Diemer, Emma Lou
Dinerstein, Norman

Erb, Donald J.
Erickson, Elaine M.

Felciano, Richard
Fox, Fred
Frackenpohl, Arthur
Freed, Arnold
Fussell, Charles

Giron, Arsenio
Glass, Philip

Hennagin, Michael

Jarrett, Jack M.
Jenkins, Joseph Willcox
Jenni, Donald
Johnston, Jack R.
Jones, Robert W.

Kennedy, John Brodbin
Keyes, Nelson H.
Korte, Karl
Kosteck, Gregory W.
Kroeger, Karl
Kurtz, James L.

Lamb, John David
Lane, Richard
Lawhead, Donaldson Vaughn
Lombardo, Robert M.
LoPresti, Ronald

Mailman, Martin
Martirano, Salvatore J.
Maves, David W.
Miller, Lewis M.
Mofsenson, Joel
Morrill, Dexter
Muczynski, Robert
Myers, Robert

Newman, Theodore S.

Owen, Harold

Peck, Russell J.
Penna, Joseph
Pierce, V. Brent

Rhodes, Phillip
Riley, Dennis

Schickele, Peter
Skolnik, Walter
Southers, Leroy W., Jr.
Stewart, Kensey D.
Susa, Conrad S.

Tcimpidis, David
Thomson, William
Tubb, Monte

Valente, William E.
Vercoe, Barry

Washburn, Robert
Wernick, Richard
White, Michael
Widdoes, Lawrence W.

Zupko, Ramon

85 DAVIES, HUGH, compiler   Répertoire International des Musiques Electroacoustiques. International Electronic Music Catalog. A cooperative publication of Le Groupe de Recherches Musicales de l'O.R.T.F., Paris, and The Independent Electronic Music Center, Inc., Trumansburg, N.Y.   Cambridge, Mass.: The M.I.T. Press (distributor), 1968   xxx, 330p   preface   appendices   indices (composers; general) (reviewed *Inter-American Institute for Musical Research Yearbook* 5:104-5 1969)

This comprehensive list (in French and English) of electronic works is arranged geographically. The large U.S. section (p169-235) is arranged by state, city, and then by studio within each city. Information given for each work: composer, title, function (concert piece, ballet, etc.), date, duration, technical data, cross-references to the appendices for further details, and notes (usually dealing with the availability of unpublished compositions).

The excellent appendices include discographies, tape-list, directory of permanent studios, and others. A book of high quality.

86　**EDMUNDS, JOHN, and GORDON BOELZNER**　Some Twentieth Century American Composers; A Selective Bibliography　New York: The New York Public Library (reviewed *Music Review* 21:337-8 Nov 1960)

  Vol. I With an Introductory Essay by Peter Yates. 1959 [Reprinted with additions and corrections from the *Bulletin of The New York Public Library,* July, August 1959] 57p　preface　index

  Vol. II With an Introductory Essay by Nicolas Slonimsky. 1960 [Reprinted with additions from the *Bulletin of The New York Public Library,* July 1960] 55p　preface　appendices ("Composers in Standard Reference Works" "Composers Not Listed in Standard Reference Works")　index

The best single source in its chosen area. Lists three types of literary material: writings about the composer; writings about his works; writings by the composer. Composers were contacted by Edmunds for verification and amplification of the lists. Magnificent portrait photos were taken especially for the publication by William and Gwen Sloan.

Vol I	Brant, Henry	Ives, Charles
	Cage, John	Partch, Virgil
	Carter, Elliott	Riegger, Wallingford
	Copland, Aaron	Ruggles, Carl
	Cowell, Henry	Sessions, Roger
	Harris, Roy	Thomson, Virgil
	Harrison, Lou	Varèse, Edgard
	Hovhaness, Alan	
Vol II	Barber, Samuel	Hanson, Howard
	Bernstein, Leonard	Kirchner, Leon
	Blitzstein, Marc	Moore, Douglas
	Creston, Paul	Piston, Walter
	Dello Joio, Norman	Porter, Quincy
	Diamond, David	Schuman, William
	Foss, Lukas	Thompson, Randall
	Glanville-Hicks, Peggy	Weber, Ben

87 GOSS, MADELEINE   Modern Music-Makers; Contemporary American Composers
New York: E. P. Dutton & Co., 1952   499p   foreword   (R Greenwood Press)
(reviewed *Notes* 9:607-8 Sept 1952)

This standard work is devoted to 37 composers, most of them from the first 20th-century generation. Each composer is dealt with in a separate "chapter" which includes photo, facsimile sample of music manuscript, list of works, chronology of important events, and a fairly detailed biography. Goss's work is polite and quite well done.

The 37 composers are:

Antheil, George	Hanson, Howard
Barber, Samuel	Harris, Roy
Bauer, Marion	Howe, Mary
Bennett, Robert Russell	Ives, Charles
Bergsma, William	McDonald, Harl
Bernstein, Leonard	Moore, Douglas
Blitzstein, Marc	Piston, Walter
Branscombe, Gena	Riegger, Wallingford
Britain, Radie	Rogers, Bernard
Carpenter, John Alden	Ruggles, Carl
Copland, Aaron	Schuman, William
Cowell, Henry	Sessions, Roger
Creston, Paul	Shapero, Harold
Daniels, Mabel	Sowerby, Leo
Dello Joio, Norman	Still, William Grant
Diamond, David	Talma, Louise
Foss, Lukas	Taylor, Deems
Gould, Morton	Thomson, Virgil
Gruenberg, Louis	

88 HOWARD, JOHN TASKER   Our Contemporary Composers; American Music in the Twentieth Century With the assistance of Arthur Mendel   New York: Thomas Y. Crowell, 1941   xv, 447p   preface   photos   appendix ("A Selected List of Books . . ."; "Recorded works . . ."; 12 other lists)   index

The companion to the author's **Our American Music (18).** Well-researched reportage on the careers of a large number of the earlier generation of 20th-century U.S. composers (and a few younger ones, too). It is dated, of course, but still good to have around. The photos are superb and the lists in the appendix are more than interesting.

Dislike: the misleading subtitle, considering that the book was written in the 1930s.

Like: the sub-heading on p241—("Unicorn and Lion"), which refers to Ruggles and Ives (it was Lawrence Gilman who called Ruggles "the first unicorn to enter American music").

89 PAN AMERICAN UNION. CULTURAL AFFAIRS DEPT. Compositores de America; Datos biograficos y catalogos de sur obras. **Composers of the Americas; Biographical data and catalogs of their works** Washington: Sección de Musica, Departamento de Asuntos Culturales, Union Panamericana vol. 1-   ; 1955-

A volume has been issued each year since 1955.

Each yearly issue covers from three to about nineteen contemporary composers. "In addition to the title, date of composition, duration of performance and the name of the publisher, each catalog includes biographical data, a photograph and a facsimile of a page of the composer's manuscript"—(introduction). Each issue contains an index to all previous numbers in the series. Excellent.

The following is a list of all U.S. composers in the series through vol. 16 (1970); the number after each name indicates the volume in which the coverage appears:

Antonini, Alfredo	15	Blitzstein, Marc	5
		Bloch, Ernest	9
Babbitt, Milton	12	Brant, Henry	6
Bales, Richard	15	Brown, Earle	12
Ballou, Esther	9		
Barber, Samuel	5	Cage, John	8
Beglarian, Grant	14	Carter, Elliott	5
Bergsma, William	6	Cazden, Norman	15
Bernstein, Leonard	6	Chou, Wen-chung	15
Binkerd, Gordon	16	Coker, Wilson	9

Copland, Aaron	1	La Montaine, John	9
Corigliano, John	9	Layton, Billy Jim	9
Cowell, Henry	2	Lees, Benjamin	12
Crumb, George	15	Lopatnikoff, Nikolai	12
Custer, Arthur	15	Luening, Otto	7
Dello Joio, Norman	9	McBride, Robert	9
Diamond, David	13	Mennin, Peter	5
Donato, Anthony	15	Muczynski, Robert	9
Donovan, Richard	15		
Dougherty, Celius	9		
		Parris, Robert	10
Evett, Robert	10	Partch, Harry	5
		Perle, George	15
Fine, Irving	6	Persichetti, Vincent	14
Finney, Ross Lee	11	Pimsleur, Solomon	13
Flanagan, William	12	Pinkham, Daniel	12
Fletcher, Grant	7	Piston, Walter	4
Foss, Lukas	7	Porter, Quincy	4
		Powell, Mel	9
Glanville-Hicks, Peggy	13		
Gottlieb, Jack	9	Read, Gardner	8
Gould, Morton	6	Riegger, Wallingford	7
Gutche, Gene	15	Rochberg, George	10
		Roger, Kurt G.	15
Hanson, Howard	5	Rogers, Bernard	10
Harrison, Lou	8	Rorem, Ned	12
Hovhaness, Alan	11		
		Schuller, Gunther	10
Imbrie, Andrew	12	Schuman, William	5
Ives, Charles	2	Seeger, Ruth Crawford	2
		Slonimsky, Nicolas	15
Kay, Ulysses	7	Spiess, Claudio	15
Kelly, Robert	13	Stevens, Halsey	11
Kirchner, Leon	7	Still, William Grant	5
Kohs, Ellis B.	15	Surinach, Carlos	9

Thomson, Virgil	3	Wagner, Joseph	12
Toch, Ernst	7	Waldrop, Gid	6
Trimble, Lester	10	Ward, Robert	9
Turok, Paul	16	Weber, Ben	9
		White, Michael	9
Ussachevsky, Vladimir	9	Whittenberg, Charles	15
Van Vactor, David	9	Yardumian, Richard	11
Vincent, John	8		

90 REIS, CLAIRE Composers in America; Biographical Sketches of Living Composers with a Record of Their Works 1912-1937 New York: Macmillan, 1938 270p

_____. [Subtitle of this ed. omits 1912-1937] Rev. and enl. ed. 1947 xvi, 339p foreword "A Supplementary List of Composers" p395-99

The 1947 edition provides brief sketches of over 300 native and foreign-born composers and lists of their works. It is authoritative for the period it deals with. While the earlier edition includes fewer composers, some in it are omitted from the 1947 edition, having died between the two. It is best, then, to have both editions if possible.

Ms. Reis was a founder and, for 25 years, the guiding force of the League of Composers, the important American organization dedicated to commissioning and performing new music.

INDEX

(References are to item-numbers, not to pages)

Eldridge, Roy   57
Ellington, Edward ("Duke")   3   49   57   58d
Ellinwood, Leonard   1   77
Elson, Arthur   3   15   19
Elson, Louis C.   15
Emery, Stephen   5
Emmett, Daniel   5
Engel, Carl   3
Engel, Lehman   61
Erb, Donald J.   84
Erickson, Elaine M.   84
Evans, Charles   9
Evans, Gil   51
Evett, Robert   89
Ewen, David   62

Fabian   68
Fairlamb, James R.   5
Farrell, Eileen   3
Farwell, Arthur   16
Feather, Leonard   49
Felciano, Richard   84
Feliciano, José   3
Fiedler, Arthur   3
Fine, Irving   89
Finney, Ross Lee   89
Fisk Jubilee Singers, The   43
Fitzgerald, Ella   83
Flanagan, William   89
Fletcher, Grant   89
Foote, Arthur   5
Ford, Tennessee Ernie   3
Foss, Lukas   3   86   87   89
Foster, Stephen   5   15
Fox, Fred   84
Fox, Virgil   3
Frackenpohl, Arthur   84
Francis, Connie   3

Franklin, Aretha   3
Fredericks, Vic   63
Freed, Arnold   84
Freeman, Harry Lawrence   28
Freeman, Larry   60a   60d
Friml, Rudolf   65
Fry, William Henry   5   20
Fuld, James J.   7   64
Fussell, Charles   84

Ganss, Henry   5
Garland, Judy   3
Gentry, Linnell   32
Georgia Minstrels, The   43
Gershwin, George   5   65   75
Gershwin, Ira   3
Gerson, Robert A.   25
Gilbert, Henry F.   5   16
Gilchrist, William   5
Gillespie, John ("Dizzy")   3   57   58a
Gilman, Lawrence   88
Giron, Arsenio   84
Gitler, Ira   58a
Giuffre, Jimmy   51
Glanville-Hicks, Peggy   83   86   89
Glass, Philip   84
Godrich, John   50
Goldberg, Joe   58b
Goldblatt, Burt   37
Goldkette, Jean   58d
Goldmark, Rubin   5
Goodman, Benny   3   49   57   58c
Gordon, Dexter   58a
Gorin, Igor   3
Goss, Madeleine   87
Gottlieb, Jack   89
Gottschalk, Louis Moreau   5   20
Gould, Morton   3   79   87   89

Hsio Wen Shih   58d
Hughes, Rupert   19
Humiston, William Henry   5
Hurok, Sol   3
Hutton, Betty   3

Imbrie, Andrew   89
Ingalls, Jeremiah   2
Ives, Burl   3
Ives, Charles   3   86   87   88   89

Jackson, George K.   5   26
Jackson, Mahalia   3   40
Jackson, Milt   51
James, Edward T.   5
James, Skip   45
Janes, Walter   2
Janis, Byron   3
Janis, Harriet   44
Jarrett, Jack M.   84
Jefferson, Blind Lemon   45
Jenkins, Joseph Willcox   84
Jenks, Stephen   2
Jenni, Donald   84
Jepson, Jorgen Grunnet   52
Jeter, Rev. Claude   40
Johns, Clayton   5
Johnson, Allen   5
Johnson, Edward   3
Johnson, H. Earle   26
Johnson, Hall   3
Johnson, J. J.   51   58a
Johnson, James P.   58c   70
Johnson, John Rosamond   1
Johnson, Robert   45
Johnson, Willie Gary ("Bunk")   58f
Johnston, Jack R.   84

Jolson, Al   3
Jones, F. O.   10
Jones, LeRoi   3
Jones, Quincy   51
Jones, Robert W.   84
Joplin, Janis   3
Joplin, Scott   44
Jubilee Singers, The Fisk (see
    Fisk Jubilee Singers)

Kahn, Ed   38
Kahn, Gus   3
Kaiser, Alois   5
Kalmar, Bert   70
Kandel, Laing Ned   68
Kapell, William   3
Kay, Beatrice   3
Kay, Ulysses   89
Keepnews, Orrin   53
Keller, Matthias   2   5
Kelley, Edgar Stillman   3
Kelly, Robert   89
Kennedy, John Brodbin   84
Kern, Jerome   3   65   75
Keyes, Joe   48
Keyes, Nelson H.   84
Killian, Al   48
Kimball, Jacob   2
Kingsley, George   2
Kinkeldey, Otto   26
Kirby, John   58d
Kirchner, Leon   3   86   89
Kirsten, Dorothy   3
Kitt, Eartha   3
Klein, Bruno   5
Knippers, Ottis J.   27
Koemmenich, Louis   5
Kohs, Ellis B.   89

Richard Jackson was born in New Orleans, Louisiana, where he did undergraduate work at Loyola University (B.M.) and graduate work at Tulane (M.A.). His studies in American music, culminating in a thesis, "The Operas of Gertrude Stein and Virgil Thomson," were supervised by Gilbert Chase. In New York he attended Pratt Institute (M.L.S.) and worked at the New School for Social Research. He became Head of the Americana Collection in The New York Public Library's Music Division in 1965.

The Institute for Studies in American Music is a division of the Brooklyn College Department of Music. Established in 1971, the Institute is a research and information center for studies in American music. Through publication of its own and others' research projects, the Institute aims to contribute to the growing field of American-music studies.